Bloody

Bloody

The Rhymes of Crime

Versicles

Jonathan Goodman

Foreword by

William H. Hildebrand

The Kent State

University Press

Kent, Ohio, and

London, England

Library of Congress Catalog Card Number 92-26985
ISBN 0-87338-470-9
Manufactured in the United States of America

Revised edition. Previously published in Great Britain by
David & Charles (Publishers) Limited, and in the U.S.A. by
St. Martin's Press, Inc., New York, copyright Jonathan Good-
man, 1971.

Library of Congress Cataloging-in-Publication Data
Goodman, Jonathan.
      Bloody versicles : the rhymes of crime / Jonathan Goodman ;
   foreword by William H. Hildebrand. —Rev. ed.
          p.   cm.
      Includes index.
      ISBN 0–87338–470–9 (alk. paper) ∞
      1. English poetry—History and criticism.   2. Crime—Great
   Britain—History—Poetry.   3. Crime—United States—History—
   Poetry.   4. American poetry—History and criticism.   5. Criminals in
   literature.   6. Crime in literature.   I. Title.
   PR508.C79G66   1993
   821.008'0355—dc20   92–26985

British Library Cataloging-in-Publication data are available.

Once again for Susan

Contents

List of Illustrations

Lives of great crooks all remind us,
We may do a stretch of time;
And, departing, leave behind us
Thumb-prints in the books of crime.

Parody of a stanza from
Longfellow's *A Psalm of Life*

Foreword

Like its author, *Bloody Versicles* is an original.

It is an anthology of amusing, informative doggerel about true crimes committed in the United States and Great Britain over the last two centuries or so. As such, there is nothing quite like it. But its true distinction is in the canny contexts—really introductions-cum-commentaries—in which Goodman sets his "crhymes." They are so stamped with his unique authority as a collector and antiquarian and historian of crime that they become autonomous brief histories of the deeds themselves—as well as of the society they at once violated and expressed. And they are colorfully illustrated with precise word-pictures of the malefactors in all their vainglory. *Bloody Versicles* has something for every taste!

Readers with a primarily literary or anthropological interest will find a fresh store of folk art, part of a tradition reaching back to the broadsheet ballads that were the poor person's newspapers from the sixteenth to the nineteenth centuries. One of my favorites, a theological couplet that might have been written by a Miltonized Larry Hart, was inspired by Isaac Sawtell's murder of his brother Hiram in the 1890s in New Hampshire:

> Two brothers in our town did dwell;
> Hiram sought heaven, but Isaac Sawtell.

Eminent literary names decorate the text as well, from Lamb and Dickens to Oscar Wilde and Cole Porter. And Goodman even salutes a disturbing notion raised by the weight of some of his entries—the possibility of a deeper link between poetry and murder than most poetry lovers (save, of course, the wives of certain poets) would care to think about.

And readers inclined toward the psychology and sociology of crime will take special delight in the commentaries—especially the notes appliquéing them. If one benchmark of a historian's mastery of his craft is his handling of endnotes, then on this count alone Goodman ranks very high indeed. His notes are never merely occasions for the freeze-drying of indigestible morsels of data. With his deft hand and keen eye for what he has called the "connectedness" of things, he makes truffles from trifles. Three cases in point: commenting on the eating habits of murderees (as F. Tennyson Jesse called victims), he posits a link between their diets and the way they die; he specifies "a four foot drop [as] dead right" for hanging a person of twelve stone; and he informs us that incest did not become a crime in English law until 1900, when the Punishment of Incest Act was passed.

Finally, readers with an appetite for mayhem and murder, whether fictive or true, will find fresh food in Goodman's exact and elegant accounts of crimes both notorious and obscure. His summaries are models of the economy of wit: "Despite Thurtell's long and impassioned speech, ending with a plea not to upset his parents by having him hanged, the jury found him guilty and he was executed outside Hertford prison in January 1824." And he has a special gift for the arresting detail, telling us that at least until the end of the nineteenth century police on the Arran Isles would bury a murderer's shoes in order to discourage his ghost from walking about.

Bloody Versicles belongs to that species of social history called, accurately if inelegantly, true crime, which has never been more widely popular, nor more widely malpracticed, than it is at present, when a savage murder seems somehow unfinished until at least two more-or-less "factual" retellings are available at the checkout counter. The general estate of his extravagant brainchild would surely fascinate Thomas De-Quincey, its improbable father—*fascinate* in the exact sense. Its prosperity would attract him even as its bad taste would alarm, thus immobilizing him in that delicious state of moral and spiritual stasis best suited to indulging the presiding passion of his life, daydreaming. Although one might expect to find an understanding of the reasons for the enormous popularity of accounts of true—that is, real—crimes in historiography or literary realism, it would be far wiser to rummage around in the dark humus from which it sprang: romanticism.

True crime is one of the few kinds of literature whose lineage and birth are matters of public record. In 1827 Thomas DeQuincey, a diminutive, delicate, and down-at-the-soul-and-heel literary journalist of high ambition and low achievement—the sensational *Confessions of an English Opium-Eater* (1822) having come from trading on his conspicuous vice—published in *Blackwell's Magazine* the first installment of his essay *On Murder Considered as One of the Fine Arts,* the second and third appearing in 1839 and 1854 respectively. Writing in the baroque musical style he had worked hard to perfect—all arpeggios and conceits, rallentandos and paradoxes—DeQuincey argued, with tongue only half in cheek, for the cultivation of our natural taste for violence, a sort of training up of the sensations on the trellis of aestheticism, to produce a sensibility capable of collecting and savoring a "good murder"—much as one would, say, appreciate a Raphael nude on the wall. After all, he happily observed, "something more goes to the composition of a fine murder than two blockheads to be killed and to kill—a purse—and a dark lane." Design, grouping, light and shade, and of course poetry and sentiment—all are essential ingredients. So, too, time and style, which alone can "tranquillize" the actual grief, anesthetize the human hurt, by providing the impersonal detachment of aesthetic distance so essential to enjoying the fine arts. Proximity always spoils pleasure for the true romantic, which DeQuincey certainly was.

His theory was grounded in a key romantic conception of art as an anodyne for ennui. The mental image fashioned by the imagination displaces the void within the self, thus enabling it, in Byron's words, to live, however briefly, "a being more intense." It was this passion for ever greater intensities of experience, which the inner dialectic of romanticism tended to exalt into an absolute value, that made murder—and the genre of true crime—a matter of romance for DeQuincey. And, just as he transposed the religious confession of St. Augustine into a peculiarly romantic prose-chorale to the god of his own idolatry, opium, so, too, he volatilized the generally benign personal essay of Lamb, Hazlitt, and Hunt into a species of historiography.

This concern for the second-hand life of visionary experience sprang from the desperate hope romanticism staked on the imagination as the Promethean power of creativity that made the artist's own suffering self his true heroic subject, as well as a competitor with the discredited Creator of traditional faith. But, because the imagination is a morally neutral medium, dissimulating in order to simulate, its conceptions have the deceptive power to make one confuse ideality with actuality. As punishment for seeing Diana naked, Acteon was turned into a stag and devoured by his own hounds. In their exuberant moments a Shelley or a Keats could soar on fancy's wings toward bright sublimities of beauty—until the afflatus would wane or the nightingale fly off, leaving him forlorn, alone with the "sole self." Perversely, however, the horror of that self, the solitary ego, had its own attractions. Its dark declivities could quicken intensities of visionary experience that would displace the humdrummery of actual, daily life just as effectively as aerial shapes of loveliness. The energy of horror, in fact, ultimately proved greater than that of bliss—or, more accurately, became indistinguishable from it, as the Decadents discovered later in the century. Whereas the worst thing the dream girl could do was leave one forlorn, the corrupt beauty of Medusa could petrify the very soul.

That DeQuincey's ruminations on the aesthetics of murder are, for all their wit, intended as a serious contribution to the literature of dark romanticism—of the same order as *Manfred* or *The Cenci*—is apparent in his portrait of the "good murderer." DeQuincey presents him as an actor whose performance transforms a drab shop or bedroom into a mise en scène. Murder is an art too exalted for a brute or a crime-hardened dullard. So DeQuincey's murderer must be exceptional in his powers and blameless in his life: "The higher the social status, the wider the learning, the more noticeable the odour of sanctity in which he has lived his life, the more interesting the crime," which partly suggests why the Wallace case is England's classic murder and the Lizzie Borden case is ours. But what is his subtext here? DeQuincey implies that the fascination, the "mystery" of the good murderer's *motive* has the power to release the imagination, licensing it to dream down into the Piranesi architecture of the depths, and in those dark turnings perhaps meet one's own unburied self.

DeQuincey's most detailed portrait of the good murderer, drawn from life, is in his account of the Ratcliffe Highway murderer John Williams who terrorized London in 1812. DeQuincey envisions him as "one solitary insulated individual" who "asserted his own supremacy over all the children of Cain"—an anticipation of Dostoyevski's Great Sinner. He is an "artist" who sets about producing "a murder of quality" as an ultimate act of romantic self-assertion. (DeQuincey's metaphors look ahead rather disturbingly to the contemporary performance artist.) Of the two likeliest motives authorities postulated for Williams's deed—thwarted love for the first victim's pretty wife or desire for monetary gain—DeQuincey chooses, of course, the romantic one. But, going beyond revenge, he speculates that Williams's secret motive was his thirst for artistic recognition, the fame of having slaughtered the whole household, husband, wife, baby—thus forcing the "poor vanquished imagination" of the city to sink "powerless before the fascinating rattlesnake eye of the murderer." And, as his impressions of the murderer become more hectic and hypnagogic, DeQuincey turns him into Medusa's head. In this fashion a very real murderer becomes an allegory of the romantic ego in its extremity of pride, the autonomous self that, as Byron said, could make a Heaven of Hell or a Hell of Heaven, but somehow always chose the latter.

Although DeQuincey's passion for the romance of murder strongly influenced the Victorian novel of Dickens, Collins, and Sheridan Le Fanu, true crime did not begin to be practiced in its highest form, as history, until the first few decades of the twentieth century. In 1913 the Scots solicitor William Roughead began publishing riveting (to Henry James, among others) accounts of the good murders his countrymen produced so prodigally—a good one every five years, he said. Though he lacked DeQuincey's resonant style and genius for psychological impressionism, in his wit and his reading of what DeQuincey called the "hieroglyphics" of a case, he was the equal of his master, and his superior in all matters forensic. His younger, American contemporary, Edmund Pearson, soon began to turn out his lapidary studies in scarlet. A bibliophile and librarian, Pearson brought wide learning and equally wide biases to bear on contemporary and historical cases, especially the Borden murders, that caught his curious eye. The twenties and thirties produced several other worthy practioners: F. Tennyson Jesse, the DeQuinceyesque stylist William Bolitho, and novelist John Dickson Carr, whose *The Murder of Sir Edmund Godfrey* is a masterpiece.

Meanwhile, a force was at work—the combined energy radiating from the Notable British and Scottish Trials series, which coupled expert introductory essays with generous portions of trial testimony—to shift the center of gravity toward that respect for the order of evidence and a disinterested view of the "mute facts," which, DeQuincey said, enables them to be "read into their true construction." This tended to purge the true-crime form of the genial impressionism it had inherited from its parent, the personal essay. But a thoroughgoing history is beyond my present brief, and, besides, I want to avoid having to comment on the baleful effects of Capote's *In Cold Blood* and Mailer's *The Executioner's Song,* works of "faction" that, though wildly popular and praised, lacked the nerve to be fiction and the discipline to be factual histories.

The foregoing remarks will, I trust, serve as proper backdrop for introducing the author of *Bloody Versicles.* Jonathan Goodman is, as Jacques Barzun has written, the "greatest living master of the true-crime literature." I would argue that he is the best ever. He is also, as his colleague and friend Albert Borowitz has said, a great detective.

Goodman was a young theatrical producer with a few crime novels and a book of verse under his belt when, doing repertory at the Playhouse in Liverpool, he went with some friends, after curtain, to see the drab house in the suburb of

Anfield where Mrs. Wallace had been murdered without apparent motive in 1931. This lark was, to change the figure, the vise that turned Goodman's head irredeemably toward crime. Intrigued, he started reading up on the case. The more he read, the more puzzling it became—until at last nothing would do but he must research it thoroughly and write about it. What he had really decided to do was solve the murder—a deplorably presumptuous decision, surely, when one remembers that the Wallace mystery had confounded the best efforts of more crime students than any other English case.

Goodman's *The Killing of Julia Wallace* (1969) proved to be the most compelling of all studies of the thirty-eight-year-old perplex. The jury had found Wallace guilty; the appeals court found him innocent, holding that the verdict was not supported by the evidence. As James Agate said: "Either the murderer was Wallace or it wasn't. If it wasn't, then here at last is the perfect murder." If perfect means unsolvable, Agate was wrong. Goodman solved it. And he did it by old-fashioned scholarship combined with a born detective's powers of reason and perception. He studied the scene and its maps; he returned to the original documents and records that constituted the body of evidence, something no other writer had done. And he turned up new evidence, interviewed survivors, and pored over the intricacies of the Liverpool tram and phone systems. Ultimately, he was able to prove Wallace innocent and to discover, interview, and eventually identify the real murderer. A stunning accomplishment, by any standard.

All of Goodman's subsequent work has been of the same high order and infused with the same devotion to justice and truth. In *The Burning of Evelyn Foster* (1977), *The Stabbing of George Harry Storrs* (1983), *The Slaying of Joseph Bowne Elwell* (1987), and *The Passing of Starr Faithful* (1990) he has given his readers the pleasures of first-rate mysteries in the form of first-rate social histories.

Jacques Barzun has commented that Goodman's chief contribution to true-crime literature is his book-length studies, which combine the virtues of the long, ruminative personal essay of the Roughead sort, at the one extreme, and the "full-blown report of a trial" of the Notable Trial series, at the other extreme. Goodman is master of a demanding art to which he brings all the virtues of intelligence and learning that his predecessors had in abundance—plus a few none of them enjoyed. His powers of analysis and his keen eye for patterns—the "connectedness" of all things relative to human beings—and his understanding of the proper uses and abuses of logic are first rate. His prose style—suave, witty, sure-footed, resonant in its range of reference—reflects a deeply serious nature, one free of romantic sentimentalism toward murderers and scornful of all theorists of the human heart whose systems are too sophisticated to let them see evil when it is staring them in the face.

WILLIAM H. HILDEBRAND

Introduction

Most people at one time or another, or as a lifelong obsession, make a collection of something or other: fading butterflies, old masters, Valentine cards, lapis lazuli—even (and I am thinking, of course, of John Reginald Halliday Christie) pubic hairs; the list is almost as long as the number of things produced by human ingenuity and evolutionary process. Of my several hobbies, the one that costs me least and gives me certainly as much pleasure as the others is the collection of crhymes (or "bloody versicles," as William Roughead called verses and ballads about crimes and criminals).

The crhymes in this book are merely representative; there are hundreds more. Sadly (so it seems to me, though I'm sure that some sociologists would think it a cause for celebration), crhyming is a dying, near dead, "art." Protest songsters, the obvious candidates to continue the tradition, hardly comment upon crime. The trouble, I suppose, is that protest has become indiscriminate; these days, so many things are considered protest-worthy, and the choice between protesting against the sending of a sports team to South Africa, the sending of deep-frozen puppies to the Philippines, and the sending of a person to prison is settled by mental coin-tossing rather than by the weighing of pet aversions.

With exceptions that will be obvious to the reader, the verses in this anthology should not be taken too seriously, either as literature (which they do not pretend to be) or as altogether truthful accounts of lives, deaths, or events. Most crhymesters take full advantage of poetic license; they have few qualms about embroidering the facts, and even inventing some, to brighten a dull crime, and are quite prepared to sacrifice truth to a rhyme (an example of this can be found in the

Lizzie Borden quatrain: no one counted the number of times Mr. Borden's head had been whacked—or Mrs. Borden's, for that matter—but a rhyme was needed for "done," and "forty-one" fitted nicely). Rather than speckle the book with corrective footnotes, I have drawn attention to errors only when they pervert the overall story of a crime or the true picture of a criminal.

Whenever possible, I have let the crhymes speak for themselves. The introductions and interruptions can be skipped if the background is known to the reader.

Some general conclusions can be drawn from the way in which the style and content of the verses change with changes in life and law; but anyone who is interested in playing this sort of guessing game should beware of hidden traps and remember that the path of inductive reasoning is strewn with red herrings: just as it would be false to assume from the popular songs of the thirties that the moon shone in June more often in that decade than in others, it would be wrong to think, simply on the evidence of repetition, that the early years of the nineteenth century were bad ones for mothers (broken-hearted) and loved ones (forever parted). Fashions in word-rhymes change as often as fashions in hemlines, and I venture to say that only a quack psychologist would attempt to explain why.

Of the four main categories of crhyme, the broadsheet ballad is the most homogeneous in terms of form, content, and purpose. Produced in large quantities from the sixteenth to the nineteenth century, broadsheets—single sheets of flimsy paper printed on one side—contain all the ingredients of a modern printer's nightmare, with wrong fonts, literals, transpositions, and slanting lines crowding between the haphazard margins. They were the popular journalism of the day, recording, usually with a combination of report and ballad, sometimes with ballad alone, every important or interesting event—and, during "silly seasons," events of no consequence at all. (It is said, not without dispute, that the word "catchpenny" derives from broadsheets that made a mountain of copy out of a mole-hill of news.) The crime broadsheets, with their tut-tutting moral tone giving the excuse for a welter of gory details, are the ancestors of our mass-circulation Sunday newspapers. In the last half of the nineteenth century, the broadsheet ballad was gradually replaced by the music-hall song, but ballads still appeared in the twentieth century to record big occasions such as the funeral of Edward VII and sensational trials such as that of Bennett.

Jemmy Catnach is the best-remembered broadsheet printer. The son of a Northumberland printer, he started business on his own account in 1813–14 at 2 Monmouth Court, Seven Dials, London, setting up scraps of type and secondhand woodcuts to print little duodecimo chapbooks (formed of sheets folded so as to make twelve leaves) and broadsheets. He paid his writers half-a-crown a ballad. Catnach's success over the next twenty-five years (he retired in 1838, having "made a competence" of some £5000—which, going by indices of inflation, would be worth about £170,000 now) seems to have been based as much on ingenuity as industry; following the murder of William Weare, a crime from which he is said to have reaped £500 in pennies, he produced one broadsheet that was headed "Weare Alive Again," afterwards explaining to deceived customers that by a typographical error no space had been left after "We."

Most of my own favorite crhymes are in the "anonymous amateur" category. Almost invariably circulated by word of mouth (which explains how some of them acquire as many as half a dozen variations), the motives behind their origin are so various that it is impossible to cite a common creative factor; they are born out of anger, belief in a person's guilt or innocence, acceptance of a theory, fascination at some piquant detail in a case. Some, of course, are simply written for fun, or owe their inspiration to the fortuitous mingling in the mind of two rhyming or similar-sounding words ("Wood"/ "wouldn't," "Young"/"hung"—page 69). Many are composed during an investigation, before a charge has been brought, and are no more than rumors in verse; although often far from the truth, they can shed interesting light on the atmosphere surrounding a case and on the public's attitude to the protagonist (the verses on page 20 go a long way towards explaining the odd verdict at the Wallace trial). Parody is a favorite device, with parodies of poems and hymns in the nineteenth century and of popular songs in the twentieth, and these are particularly evocative of the period.

In her preface to *Encyclopaedia of Murder* (1961), Mrs. Pat Pitman notes "the remarkable number of times some such phrases as, 'He fancied himself a poet' or 'During the trial he composed various verses . . .' will occur in accounts of even unlettered and brutish murderers." With the addition of the phrase, "This verse is *said to be* the work of such-and-such a criminal," a third category is explained. Some United States criminologists, struck by the number of poetic murderers, are searching for a connection between the verse urge and the urge to kill. I feel that there would be far better reason for research if the facts were the other way around—if it could be shown that hardly any murderers write verse; negative evidence, like the Sherlock Holmes dog that did not bark in the night, is often the most revealing.

By no means all crhymes are written by hacks or amateurs, and so a final category can be concocted from the work of good and/or professional poets and lyric writers. It is, admittedly, more of a hotch-potch category than the others, and therefore likely to offend literary insularies. I can only say that while it is true that an excess of ingenuity would be needed to fashion a link between, say, the gory gaiety of Michael Brown's "You Can't Chop your Poppa Up in Massachusetts" and the somber beauty of Housman's "The Culprit," there is no denying that both authors, judged by the standard of what they set out to achieve, are master craftsmen. I have had to omit several lyrics which rely upon their musical accompaniment for phrasing and punctuation, and so make poor, sometimes almost meaningless, reading. Perhaps the most conspicuous absentee among the poems is Wilde's "The Ballad of Reading Gaol," the subject of which is Charles Thomas Wooldridge, a trooper of the Royal Horse Guards, who was hanged in July 1896 for the murder of his unfaithful wife; that poem, which runs to 109 stanzas, is too long to be included, and it would be a shame to present it in anything less than its entirety.

There is a famous remark by Mr. Justice Maule, who inter-
rupted the presentation of a complicated case to say: "I
should like to stipulate for some sort of order. There are
plenty of them. There is the chronological, the botanical, the
metaphysical—why, even the alphabetical order would be bet-
ter than no order at all." Faced with much the same problem
as the unfortunate advocate in that case, I have chosen a di-
vision into types of crime, listed alphabetically (with the ex-
ception of the cardinal crime of murder, which must take
pride of place), and have devoted a final section to crhymes
about punishment; at the very end, alone, refusing to accept
a place among the other crhymes, is "The Ballad of John
Glaister." The two largest divisions are arranged, again alpha-
betically, under method of murder and category of larceny.
Not all the criminals are completely at home in their respec-
tive sections: for instance, the Barrow, James, and Kelly
gangs, between them, caused nearly as many deaths as all the
inhabitants of the *Murder* section put together, but their main
occupations, and the ones they are chiefly remembered for,
place them among the larcenists. I have followed this "main
occupation" rule all the way through.

Bloody Versicles

Murder

assassination,

fratricide,

infanticide,

multicide,

parricide,

uxoricide,

and just plain

homicide

THE MURDER AT FALL RIVER.

ALEXANDER B. BEARD, AUTHOR.

THE AUTHOR

The crimes we read of every day
  Cause many hearts to shiver;
But few surpass in magnitude
  The murder at Fall River.

Now Andrew Borden was a man
  Of wealth and great renown.
Quite unexpectedly did fall
  The blow that struck him down.

Upon the morn of August fourth,
  In eighteen ninety two
The neighbors heard three piercing screams
  That thrilled them through and through.

They hastened to the Borden home,
  Oh! what did they find there?
Cries of affright and deep alarm
  Broke on the morning air.

The sight they saw on entering in
  Filled each with wild dismay.
There weltering in his own life blood,
  Poor Mr. Borden lay.

His head was by a hatchet hacked
  Which took away his life,
And in her room in the same plight
  They also found his wife.

Investigations soon began
  To probe that awful crime.
It still remains a mystery
  Up to the present time.

Suspicion fell on different ones
  Amidst excitement wild;
Till they arrested Lizzie B.
  The victims' youngest child.

They placed her in the prison walls
  To let the court decide
If she was guilty of that act
  The crime of parricide.

No evidence could her convict
  The jury did agree
That it was all by far too weak
  So Lizzie was set free.

Now I have briefly told this tale
  Some points I have left out;
Up to this day in many minds
  The matter is in doubt.

This much I'll say to one and all
  Let's pray with all our might;
Whoever did that awful deed
  That God will bring to light.

Address of the Author No. 201 Winter St., West Manchester, N. H.

Murder by Axe / 1

> Lizzie Borden took an axe
> And gave her Mother forty whacks.
> When she saw what she had done,
> She gave her Father forty-one.[1]
>
> ANON.

This best-known of all crhymes, one often recited by President Theodore Roosevelt, represents the majority view on the Borden case, as does the couplet chanted by children in Fall River, Massachusetts, after the murder of Andrew Borden and his second wife, Abby, on the morning of Thursday, 4 August 1892:

> Mr. Borden he is dead,
> Lizzie hit him on the head.

But a few students of the case (notably Edward D. Radin, who puts the blame on Bridget Sullivan, the Bordens's Irish housemaid[2]) agree with the less uncharitable view expressed by A. L. Bixby during Lizzie's trial:

> *To Lizzie*
>
> There's no evidence of guilt,
> Lizzie Borden,
> That should make your spirit wilt,
> Lizzie Borden;
> Many do not think that you
> Chopped your father's head in two,
> It's so hard a thing to do,
> Lizzie Borden.

You have borne up under all,
Lizzie Borden,
With a mighty show of gall,
Lizzie Borden;
But because your nerve is stout
Does not prove beyond a doubt
That you knocked the old folks out,
Lizzie Borden.

The case has formed the basis of several novels and plays, and has even been the subject of a ballet (Agnes de Mille's *Fall River Legend*). In 1952 it reappeared in Michael Brown's song, "You Can't Chop your Poppa Up in Massachusetts," featured in Leonard Sillman's Broadway review, *New Faces:*

One hot day in old Fall River,
Mister Andrew Borden died,
And they book'd his daughter Lizzie
On a charge of homicide.
Some folks say, "She didn't do it,"
Others say, "Of course she did."
But they all agree Miss Lizzie B.
Was quite a problem kid.

'Cause you can't chop your poppa up in Massachusetts,
Not even if it's planned as a surprise.
No, you can't chop your poppa up in Massachusetts;
You know how neighbors love to criticize.

Now, she got him on the sofa,
Where he'd gone to take a snooze,
And I hope he went to heaven,
'Cause he wasn't wearing shoes.
Lizzie kind of rearranged him
With a hatchet, so they say.
And then she got her mother
In that same old-fashioned way.

But you can't chop your momma up in Massachusetts,
Not even if you're tired of her cuisine.[3]

No, you can't chop your momma up in Massachusetts;   *bloody*
If you do, you know there's bound to be a scene.   *versicles*

5

Now, it wasn't done for pleasure
And it wasn't done for spite,
And it wasn't done because the lady
Wasn't very bright.
She had always done the slightest thing
That mom and poppa bid.
They said, "Lizzie, cut it out,"
And that's exactly what she did.

But you can't chop your poppa up in Massachusetts,
And then get dressed to go out for a walk.
No, you can't chop your poppa up in Massachusetts;
Massachusetts is a far cry from New York.

NOTES

1. "This is not the way I sang it as a boy of nine or ten in Oswego, New York. The authorized version with us (sung, of course, to the tune of 'Ta-Ra-Ra-Boomdeeay') was much closer to the facts of the case:

> Lizzie Borden took an axe,
> Gave her mother forty whacks.
> Then she stood behind the door
> And gave her father forty more.

A picture in the Pearson book on the Borden trial shows the door at Mr. Borden's head and the suggestion is made in the text that the murderer could have been shielded from blood-stains by this door." George P. Meade, quoted in *True Crime Detective* (USA), Spring 1953.

Still closer to the truth in some particulars is Richard Whittington-Egan's version (in a review in *Books and Bookmen*, October 1968, of Victoria Lincoln's *A Private Disgrace: Lizzie Borden by Daylight*, Gollancz, 1968):

> Lizzie Borden took an axe
> And gave her stepma twenty whacks.
> For fear her father found out then,
> She dealt him out another ten.

2. *Lizzie Borden: The Untold Story*, Gollancz, 1961.

3. "Mrs. Borden appeared about seven, and her husband and Mr. Morse [a visiting in-law] soon following, the three breakfasted together. This breakfast was subsequently discussed at more than one legal investigation, so it may be said that according to Mr. Morse it consisted of mutton, bread, coffee, 'sugar cakes,' and bananas. The servant, who prepared the food, said that

there was *mutton-broth*, as well as mutton itself, johnny cakes, coffee, and cookies. Bridget insisted, in answer to the specific question, that to the best of her belief they had no bananas that day. At all events, for a hot morning and midsummer it was a breakfast well adapted to set the stage for a tragedy. One trembles at the thought of beginning a day in August with mutton-soup." Edmund Pearson, "The Borden Case," *Studies in Murder*, Random House, 1938.

Murder by Axe / 2

This account of a crime that took place on Friday, 11 May 1894, near Browning, Missouri, is condensed from the *Encyclopaedia of the History of Missouri:* [1]

> The Taylor brothers, William P. and George E., were prosperous and influential citizens, but were nevertheless suspected of cattle-stealing. One Gus Meeks, who lived on a farm owned by the Taylors, knew something of his landlords' affairs, and he and his family were murdered to dispose of their testimony. The killing was done with an axe, and the bodies hidden in a strawstack. Little Nellie was left for dead, but revived and made her way to a neighbor's cabin, where she told of the crime. Both Taylors were convicted of murder, and William Taylor was hanged, but George broke jail and was never recaptured. The *Columbia Missourian* reported that a hermit who died near Tulsa, Oklahoma, 8 July 1926, was identified as George Taylor. Nellie Meeks recovered and lived for many years, but she had a conspicuous "dint" in her forehead.

Nellie Meeks is said to have sung the following song as she travelled about with a carnival company in the late 1890s:

> I'm one of Mr. Meeks's little girls,
> And if you'll lend an ear,
> I'll tell you all the saddest tale
> That ever you did hear.
>
> We lived upon the Taylors's farm
> Not many miles from town,

7

One night while we was all asleep
The Taylor boys come down.

They wanted to take my papa away,
My mamma answered no,
We could not be left here alone,
But the family all could go.

We got into the wagon then
An' rode to Jenkins Hill,
An' all at once we knew not why,
But the team was standin' still.

They murdered my mamma an' papa too,
An' knocked baby in the head,
They murdered my brothers an' sisters four
An' left me there as dead.

An' now my little song you've heard,
An' the rest you all know well,
I'm left an' orphaned here alone
In this wide world to dwell.

I want you all to pray for me
That I may meet them there,
In heaven above where all is love,
There'll be no murderin' there.

NOTE

1. Edited by Howard L. Conard, Southern History Co., 1901.

Murder by
Blunt Instrument / 1

On the night of Saturday, 9 July 1864, thirty-nine years after
the inauguration of the first railway line for passenger traffic,
between Stockton and Darlington, a carriage of an all-stops
train of the North London Railway—the 9:50 from the ter-
minal Fenchurch Street to Chalk Farm—became the first
British one that was the scene of a murder. The victim,
clubbed with his own walking stick before being toppled on to
the permanent way between the stations of Hackney Wick
and Bow, was an elderly banker named Thomas Briggs. The
murder was in furtherance of robbery, the proceeds of which
were paltry: a gold watch and chain, and a pair of gold-
rimmed spectacles. The criminal had also taken Mr. Briggs's
topper—but apparently by mistake, since his own hat, low-
crowned, made of beaverskin, was lying in the blood-stained
carriage. The investigators (led by Dick Tanner, a whiz-kid in-
spector in the sixteen-strong detective department at Scot-
land Yard) got their first break on the following Monday—
from Mr. Death, a jeweller of Cheapside, who, shortly before
receiving a police notice about the stolen items, had accepted
the watch chain from a young man with a German accent in
exchange for a less splendid chain, together with a cornelian
ring priced at five shillings. Though there were offers of sub-
stantial rewards—first from Mr. Briggs's employers, then
from the government, lastly from the North London Rail-
way—it was not until the next Monday that a cab driver,
Jonathan Matthews, came forward to identify the left-behind
hat as the property of Franz Müller, a German expatriate tai-
lor who was a friend of the Matthews family, and to say that

THE

MURDER

In the Railway Train.

Air : " Riding in a Railway Train."

Listen to my song, and I will not detain you
   long,
Fresh news for you I've heard ;
Of a murder that's been done, and Muller
   is the one,
And the place where it all occure'd.
Between Stepney and Bow, they struck the
   fatal blow,
To resist he tried all in vain ;
Murdered by some prigs, was poor Mr.
   Briggs,
Whilst riding in a railway train.

Now Muller has arrived, we shall all be sur-
   prised,
To hear that it's not him on the trial ;
Give him time to repent, and prove his in-
   nocence ;
To hear the evidence give no denial ;
In America, I've heard, they have listened
   to every word,
Like England they think he is the same,
That destroyed Brigg's life, on the Saturday
   night
Whilst riding in a railway train.

Muller he did state, that he was going to
   emigrate,
Long before this dreadful tragedy ;
In the Bay of New York, where Muller was
   caught,
In the Victoria that had just come from sea,
They found the watch and hat on him, which
   looked very black ;
They had evidence to prove they were the
   same,
That poor Mr. Briggs had the night that he
   was stabb'd,
Whilst riding in a railway train.

His guilt he did deny, Death knew him with
   half an eye,
Which has banished all our hopes and fears,
When the inspector searched his trunks, he
   said he'd had the hat twelve months,
And the watch had been his for two years.
That was not true, we very well knew,
I really think Muller is to blame,
Tho' he says, He's not the one, and he's sure
   he never done,
The murder in the railway train.

I am rather now inclined to think that we
   shall find
That Muller must have had an help-mate,
For such a deed to do there must have been
   two,
To have caused Briggs to have met with
   such a fate.
Why did not the cabman say, and not stow
   the jeweller's box away,
Until Muller had cross'd the wide main ;
If he knew, 'twas very wrong, to keep the
   secret up so long,
About the murder in therailway tr ain.

When all this is proved, to Newgate he'll be
   moved,
And there to await Calcraft's hand ;
While confined in the prison, time for re-
   pentance will be given,
And good advice be placed at his command.
Let this a warning be in this land of liberty
With such foul crimes never charge your
   brain,
But if it should be him, on the gallows let
   him swing,
For the murder in the railway train.

Müller had lately given the youngest of the Matthews children a little box bearing the gilt-lettered name of Death. By the time the police got to Müller's lodgings, he had set sail for New York on the SS *Victoria*. Precursive of the transatlantic chase after Dr. Crippen (see page 91), Tanner and others, with Mr. Death among them, boarded a faster ship to New York, *The City of Manchester*, which docked days before the *Victoria*. Without help from Tanner, who, having been lionized by the American press, was fulfilling social engagements, Müller was taken into custody. Among his possessions were Mr. Briggs's watch and hat—or rather, most of the latter, for he had abbreviated the crown so as to delete identifying marks within, thereby making it more like a bowler than a topper.[1] The minute the news reached England, broadsheet versifiers, dozens of them, began composing. This is an extract from one of the compositions, "Lamentation of Franz Muller" (sans umlaut, like the rest, because the printer's font was basic):

> That fatal night I was determined,
> Poor Thomas Briggs to rob and slay,
> And in the fatal railway carriage,
> That night, I took his life away.
> His crimson gore did stain the carriage.
> I threw him from the same, alack!
> I on the railway left him bleeding,
> I robbed him of his watch and hat.

Another broadsheet verse, prophetic of the denouement, was so admired by rival publishers that they pinched it and printed it with a word changed here and, regardless of scansion, a word added there. The seventh and final stanza of one of the versions went like this:

Now Muller's caught at last, tho' he's been so very fast,
And on him they found the golden watch and hat,
Tho' on the ocean he did roam, he'd better stayed at home,
And hid himself in some small darkened crack.
Tho' he pleads his innocence, that is absolute nonsense,
For they'll hang him just as sure as he's a man,

For he got up to his rigs,[2] and murdered Mr. Briggs
While riding in a London railway train.

Following extradition proceedings, Müller was transported
back to England, where he was tried and found guilty, and
(despite German efforts to save him—one by the King of
Prussia, who sent a pleading telegram to an unheeding
Queen Victoria) executed outside Newgate Prison. Just be-
fore that, he had confessed to the crimes.

NOTES

1. Within weeks of the arrest, American hatters fashioned resemblances of
"the Müller hat"; within months, so did English ones. (The case also sparked
innovations between the lines: communication cords, and—soon plugged
because of misuse by Peeping Toms—spy holes in walls between closed
compartments.)

2. *Rigs* = illicit or illegal activities.

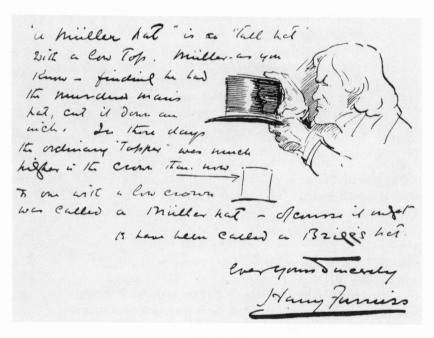

A "Muller" Hat

Murder by
Blunt Instrument / 2

If police records are to be believed, Frederick Bailey Deeming, much-travelled and many-aliased thief and swindler, did not take up murder until 1891. In the July of that year, more than making up for lost time, he killed his wife and four children. Having buried the bodies under the kitchen floor at Dinham Villa, Rainhill, near Liverpool, Deeming (whose current alias was Williams) married Miss Emily Mather and sailed with his new wife to Australia. Within a month of their arrival, Emily was dead and buried (under the bedroom floor of a house in Windsor, Melbourne), and Deeming was applying to a matrimonial agency for a replacement. Before the agency could help, however, Deeming suddenly decided to leave Melbourne, and, on a boat to Sydney, met, proposed to, and was accepted by Miss Katie Rounsfell (by then, having in the meantime changed his name from Williams to Droven or Drewen, Deeming was calling himself Baron Swanston). Leaving Miss Rounsfell in Sydney, he set off for Southern Cross to take up a job with a gold-mining company. His prospective third wife—and prospective seventh victim, no doubt—was on her way to join him when the body of wife number two was discovered. Traced to Southern Cross, Deeming was arrested, taken back to Melbourne, tried and, his insanity plea being rejected, convicted, and, on 23 May 1892, executed.

A couple of years before his names became household words, he took part in a verse competition on board a ship on which he was travelling to South America. None of his own efforts has survived, but we do have the pungent contribution of Mr. Pearce Edgecumbe, a well-known member of the Liberal Party:

And here comes Mr. Deeming,
Whose face is always beaming.

Deeming was extraordinarily protean. After his arrest for murder, a South African paper, the *Orange Leader*, commented on the multiplicity of conflicting descriptions and drawings:

> Like a tinker, like a tailor,
> Like a long and lathy draper,
> Like a murderer full of scheming,
> Big and brawny, small and slim!
>
> Like a weather-beaten sailor!
> Every illustrated paper
> Had a different kind of Deeming,
> But they all could swear to him.

There were several verses inspired by Emily's fate. The following acrostic appeared in the *Sydney Truth:*

> **E**lusive was thy dream of bliss,
> **M**urdered by him, whose lover's kiss
> **I**n England won thy heart;
> **L**ured from thy home with none to take
> **Y**our part.
>
> **W**ed to the grave, fair bride of death,
> **I**n thy last solemn sleep,
> **L**ie now at rest, while angels fair
> **L**ove's silent watches keep;
> **I**n ages yet unborn, thy name
> **A** tale of suffering shall disclose,
> **M**urdered far from thy native land,
> **S**weet peace to thee, fair English rose.

AUBURN REDMOND

Emily was buried under (inter alia) her maiden name. The gravestone bore the inscription:

> Who all her days while yet alive
> To live in honor she did strive

Till he she trusted as her guide
Without cause or warning her life denied.

Advice

To those who hereafter come reflecting
Upon this text of her sad ending:
To warn her sex of their intending,
For marrying in haste is depending
On such a fate too late for amending.

By her friend
E. THUNDERBOLT

In Australia, England, and South Africa, the countries where Deeming had spent most of his criminal career, the press devoted yards of space to his arrest and trial. Several papers enlivened the accounts with verses. A good example is "A Rhyme of the Rope," which appeared in the *Bulletin*, a New South Wales paper:

By the churches and the chapels
Where the saints in glory sing,
Sure as God made little apples,
F. B. D. has got to swing.

In England, a *Punch* contributor, tired of reading about Deeming—and tired, in particular, of the attention given to an incident in which Deeming had surreptitiously shaved off his mustache, apparently with the notion of confounding those who would be called to identify him—produced a set of verses entitled "How They Bring the Good News." The first stanza ran:

All the papers teeming
With the news of Deeming
On the shore or ship,
Telling of his tearing
Hair that he was wearing
From his upper lip.

There were several verses said to have been written by Deeming himself but probably ghosted by journalists:

> Oh, Kitty dear, Oh did you hear
> The news that's going round?
> The Baron is by law forbid
> To live on Austral ground.

☞

> As beautiful Kitty one morning was tripping
> Along the wet deck of the ship *Adelaide*,
> When I saw her I stumbled,
> Right after her tumbled,
> And before the night fell my attentions I paid.

Deeming's supposed last verse, "To God I Call," written the day before the noose silenced his muse, ended:

> My heart's love comes—my spirit parts,
> With sins my heart was beguiled,
> But now God looks with tenderness
> And claims me as his child.
> Oh, heaven, thy joyous hopes!
> The door opes—up, perplexed, I start;
> Timid, yet confident, I stand.
> Begone distrust, no more apart
> Should lovers dwell—I seize His hand
> And nestle next His heart.

Following the prison governor's refusal to hand over Deeming's brain for medical examination, the *Bulletin* expressed annoyance with the acquisitive surgeons in verses entitled "A Buried Question," which went, in part:

> Was Deeming mad, and could his brain
> Be reckoned rotten?
> What odds if he were mad or sane?
> Unopened let his skull remain,
> Whilst all the doctors rage in vain
> Till he's forgotten.

Murder by
Blunt Instrument / 3

In 1929 American-born Philip Yale Drew, a fading matinée idol who had appeared under the name of "Young Buffalo" in many silent cowboy films and starred at the Lyceum in London, was playing the part of a detective in a second-rate touring production of *The Monster*. On Saturday, 22 June, a sixty-year-old tobacconist called Alfred Oliver was struck down in his shop on Cross Street, near the County Theatre, Reading, where *The Monster* was ending a week's run; £12 (present purchasing power about £275) was stolen from the till. Several witnesses tentatively identified Drew as the "suspicious stranger" seen in the vicinity of the shop at about 6 P.M., when the murder took place; according to members of the touring company, however, Drew was in his dressing-room then. While the police, headed by the bearded Chief Inspector Berrett of Scotland Yard, tried to sort out the conflicting evidence, *The Monster* continued to traipse from town to town. On 2 October, Drew returned to Reading for the inquest— virtually "trial by coroner." The proceedings dragged on until 10 October, when the jury, after deliberating for two and three-quarter hours, returned an open verdict: "Wilful murder against some person or persons unknown." This was greeted with loud applause, and Drew returned through cheering crowds to his hotel, where he made a "curtain-call speech" from a balcony.

The show-business saying that "bad publicity is the best publicity" was certainly not true in the case of Philip Yale Drew, who found it at first difficult, soon impossible, to obtain work. He died in poverty in 1940, and is buried in an unmarked grave in Chingford Mount Cemetery, London.[1]   *17*

THEATRE ROYAL NOTTINGHAM

Proprietors - MOSS' EMPIRES, Ltd.

Managing Director
Resident Manager

Telephone 42,100.

R. H. GILLESPIE
C. B. FOUNTAINE

MONDAY, JANUARY 30th, 1928,

For Six Nights at 7.30.

MATINEE SATURDAY AT 2.

OLGA LINDO PRODUCTIONS LTD.

PRESENT

The Enormously Successful American "Thriller"

THE MONSTER

(D. LEWIN MANNERING as "Doctor Ziska")

BY CRANE WILBUR.

CHARACTERS :

" Rod " Mackenzie	PHILIP YALE DREW
Caliban (a Negro)	FRED PEASE
Alexia Bruce	LAWRENCE HANRAHAN
The Man with no face	NORMAN LESLIE
Sadie Hartley	HARRIS WAKEFIELD
Borne	PHYLLIS CRITCHERSON

MATINEE SATURDAY at 2

and

Doctor Ziska ... ... D. LEWIN MANNERING

ACT 1	.	.	.	.	.	THE LIBRARY.
ACT 2	.	.	.	.	.	THE BEDROOM.
ACT 3	.	.	.	.	THE UNDERGROUND CELLAR.

The Action of the play takes place at the present time in a house situated in a remote part of the Country, 10.30 p.m. on a stormy night. As the mystery starts with the rise of the curtain, the audience is respectfully requested to be seated punctually.

The Entire Production presented under the Personal Supervision of

MISS OLGA LINDO

(THE EMINENT LONDON ACTRESS).

Sets and Elaborate Scenery and Effects by J. PATTERSON, Surrey Theatre, London.
Electrical Installation by BRYANT & SONS, Mayfair.   The Electric Chair used in Act III. is an exact replica of the original in Sing Sing prison, New York.
Miss Marion Wakefield's Dresses by GUIVERS, Bond Street, W.

General Manager		FRANK LINDO
Stage Director	For Olga Lindo Productions, Ltd.	NORMAN LESLIE
Assistant Stage Manager		FRED BARRON

Seats booked by telephone and not claimed by 6.30 on day of performance will be sold

Doors open not later than 6.45.

BOX OFFICE AT THEATRE. Hours 10 to 9.   'Phone 42,100.

MONDAY, FEB. 6th 1928, for Six Nights at 7.30.   Matinee Saturday at 2

HERBERT   JACK

CLAYTON and WALLER

present THEIR ONLY TOURING COMPANY in

THE GIRL FRIEND

The Musical Comedy Success direct from the Palace Theatre, London.

CAST INCLUDES

JACK LEOPOLD	BABETTE ODEAL
CHARLES HANBURY	HENRY LYTTON, Junr.

and

CORA GOFFIN

DRAKE & WISE LTD. PRINTERS, CANAL STREET, NOTTINGHAM.

Giving evidence at the inquest, Drew often used the coroner's questions as cues for impromptu and entirely irrelevant speeches about his life in, and love of, the theater. At one point, asked to explain why he had stayed late at the County Theatre on the night of the murder, he described his enjoyment in watching a set being erected or taken down, then mentioned that he was writing an "atmospheric poem" about the theater. He was about to launch into a recitation, but the coroner firmly changed the subject. Just as well for Drew, perhaps, for if the jury had been forced to listen to all twenty-four stanzas of "The Theatre Speaks," they might well have returned a specific verdict. One stanza is worth quoting for its relevance to Drew the murder suspect rather than Drew the actor:

> Of actor, playwright, glory, fame—
> "What's in a name?" someone has asked.
> If passer-by be Abe or Cain,
> Suffice to say, "A man has passed."

NOTE

1. For a full account both of Drew's life and of the Reading murder, see *The Ordeal of Philip Yale Drew*, Richard Whittington-Egan, Penguin, 1989.

Murder by
Blunt Instrument / 4

A telephone call from a man calling himself R. M. Qual-
trough lured William Herbert Wallace, a fifty-two-year-old
Prudential insurance agent, from his home in the Liverpool
suburb of Anfield on the night of Tuesday, 20 January 1931.
He returned to find his wife Julia battered to death in the
front parlor. The police decided that Wallace himself had
made the telephone call as a prelude to a cunningly contrived
alibi—that he had murdered his wife before leaving the
house. And most people in Liverpool agreed, their attitude
being summed up in a parody of Baroness Orczy's "Scarlet
Pimpernel" quatrain:[1]

> They seek him here, they seek him there;
> Is he alive, do you know?
> Either in hell or the Pruden-shell,
> That damned elusive Qualtrough.

There was no scintilla of direct evidence against Wallace,
and the circumstantial evidence was equivocal. That Wallace
had no apparent motive did not deter the rumormongers,
who concocted any number of reasons why he should have
wanted his wife out of the way—including, of course, that
stock character, "the other woman":

> Willie had a mistress,
> Willie had a wife.
> He only wanted one of them,
> So Willie took a life.

Wallace was found guilty by a prejudiced Liverpool jury;
but, for the first and only time in a murder case, the Court of
Criminal Appeal quashed a verdict on the ground that "it

could not be supported having regard to the evidence." Wallace returned to Liverpool, to the house on Wolverton Street and to his old job with the Prudential; the feeling against him was still high, however, and he was forced to move to Bromborough, Cheshire, where he died eighteen months later. I believe that, in my book on the case,[2] I have proved Wallace's innocence, but the case is the classic crime puzzle, and no doubt the argument will continue.

NOTES

1. The Pimpernel verse was parodied again in November 1974, when Lord Lucan (a descendant of the one who ordered the Light Brigade to charge during the Battle of Balaclava), having made a complete mess of his life—and an incomplete mess of the lives of some others—made a dreadful botch-up of an attempt to murder his estranged wife (whom he, never one to let facts interfere with his beliefs, blamed for all of his troubles, even those brought on by a long run of bad luck at gambling, which was not only his profession but also his obsession): he entered his family's house in Belgravia, London, and in the darkness (he had not thought to bring a torch and did not dare to switch on a light), mistook Sandra Rivett, his children's nanny, for his wife—and beat her to death. Leaving London, he drove to the south coast, stopping en route at the houses of chums, and parked the car in a back street in Newhaven. That was the last trace of him. Every so often since, pop papers have reported sightings of him in far away—and far apart—places; but it is virtually certain that he boarded a cross-Channel ferry at Newhaven and "did the proper thing," namely, committed suicide—jumping overboard and not putting himself out to stay afloat. While the police were looking for him, a member of his favorite gambling club, the Clermont, made up this:

> They seek him here, they seek him there—
> The fuzz, they seek him everywhere.
> They haven't found a single clue yet
> To the whereabouts of Lord Lucan of Roulette.

> If he's not in Heaven or Hell,
> One thing's sure—his pals won't tell:
> His arrest, to them, would be bad news,
> Unless he had paid his IOUs.

2. *The Killing of Julia Wallace*, Headline, 1987.

Murder by
Blunt Instrument / 5

The kidnapping and murder of Charles Lindbergh, Jr., the twenty-month-old son of the first man to fly solo across the Atlantic, would probably never have been solved but for President Roosevelt's decision—implemented on 1 May 1933, exactly fourteen months after the abduction—that all gold valued at more than a hundred dollars should be taken out of circulation. On 18 September 1934, a New York bank teller recognized a gold certificate as part of the $50,000 paid in ransom, and the certificate was traced back, via a petrol station, to Bruno Richard Hauptmann, a thirty-six-year-old German illegal immigrant living in the Bronx, who had worked as a carpenter until a day or so after the ransom was paid. There was plenty of evidence to convict Hauptmann (including that of a timber expert, who testified that parts of the kidnapper's homemade ladder had been cut from a floorboard in Hauptmann's attic), and, after a delay that was long even by American standards, he was electrocuted on 3 April 1936.[1]

A correspondent recalls:

> In 1936 I was Cub Mistress to a pack of Wolf Cubs in a Scottish village. On asking a six-year-old new recruit to sing a song, he lustily sang the following (to the tune of "Roll Along, Covered Wagon, Roll Along"), loudly assisted by his companions:

> Roll along, Bruno Hauptmann, roll along
> To the electric chair, for that's where you belong.
> You deserve all you've got
> For stealing the baby from its cot.
> Roll along, Bruno Hauptmann, roll along.

The first Lindbergh ransom note

Dear Sir!
     Have 50,000$ ready 25000$ in 20$ bills 15000$ in 10$ bills and 10000$ in 5$ bills. Afer 2–4 days we will inform you were to deliver the mony.
     We warn you for making anyding public or for notify the Police the child is in gut care
     Indication for all letters are singnature and three holes.

When I said to the Cubs, "That is a horrible, cruel song," they said, "Aye, but we love it, miss."

(Cole Porter, who had perfected the lyric of his song "I Get a Kick Out of You" shortly before the kidnapping, felt obliged to alter the lines between "I get no kick in a plane" and "Yet I get a kick out of you"—which were "I shouldn't care for those nights in the air / That the fair Mrs. Lindbergh goes through"—to "Flying too high with some guy in the sky / Is my idea of nothing to do.")

NOTE

1. For a detailed account of the case, see *Kidnap* by George Waller (Hamish Hamilton, 1961) or, better still, *The Lindbergh Case* by Jim Fisher (Rutgers University Press, New Jersey, 1987). Don't, for heaven's sake, read the book by Ludovic Kennedy in which he tries to prove that Hauptmann was innocent, for it is peppered with errors—all of which (by complete chance, of course—of course) lend ersatz support to his notion.

Murder by Blunt Instrument, Fire-arm, Knife, and Strangulation

Found guilty of seven murders committed in the Glasgow area within two years, thirty-one-year-old Peter Manuel was hanged on 11 July 1958.[1] A habitual criminal, whose first recorded offense was at the age of eleven, when he broke into a chapel and stole from the offertory box, New York–born Manuel had some artistic talent. In 1946, shortly before he was sentenced to eight years for rape, he filled an exercise book with drawings (including one of Pierre Laval, the French Prime Minister who defected to the Nazis, with the caption, "The Man who Dared . . ."), parodies of Shakespeare ("Written by Shilliam Wakespeare"), and verses. A verse entitled simply "Moral" was flanked by drawings of two men, one haughty, the other downtrodden:

> Beware of too sublime a sense
> Of your own worth and consequence.
> The man who dreams himself so great
> And his importance of such weight
> That all around, in all that's done,
> Must move and act for him alone,
> Will learn in the school of tribulation
> The folly of his expectation.

NOTE

1. Awaiting execution, Manuel confessed to three other murders, and, after his death, a coroner's inquest found that he had committed a fourth.

Murder by Cut-throat Razor

In one of his shortest but most amusing essays,[1] Edmund Pearson relates how the efforts of New York newspaper "sob sisters" and analysts (the latter, better known today as psychiatrists, were his lifelong bêtes noires) helped to save the life of Italian-born Maria Barberi, who, in April 1895, crept up behind her lover, Domenico Cataldo, while he was playing cards in a barroom, and cut his throat with "an unpleasant, jagged razor, which looked as if it had been used not only to sharpen pencils but to open tin cans."

Pearson quotes a street ballad that was sold during the second trial (the first, with its verdict of guilty, having been denounced as a "ferocious absurdity" by tabloid newspapers, women's organizations, and Italo-American societies, and set aside by a vote-conscious governor of New York):

> 'Tis not for me to speak aloud
> On lofty themes. I tell
> As one among the lowly crowd
> How young Maria fell.
>
> Swift as a flash a glittering blade
> Across his throat she drew,
> "By you," she shrieked, "I've been betrayed:
> This vengeance is my due!"[2]
>
> Behold her now, a wounded dove:
> A native of a clime
> Where hearts are melted soon with love
> And maddened soon to crime.

1. "Sob Sisters Emerge," which appears in, among other books, one that I have edited: *The Pleasures of Murder,* Sphere, 1986.

2. In fact, Maria seems to have committed the murder without bothering to explain why. Pearson, at any rate, mentions no declaration from Miss Barberi; he does, however, refer to the victim's reaction: "Cataldo, thoroughly dismayed, rose from his chair and rushed into the street. Pausing in front of the bar-room, at the corner of Avenue A and Fourteenth Street, he remarked: 'I die!' And, falling upon the pavement, he instantly made good his statement."

Murder (?) by Drowning (?)

The Workhouse Boy
(Victorian; to the tune, "The Mistletoe Bough")

The cloth vos laid in the vorkhouse hall,
And the greatcoats hung on the vhitevash'd vall,
The paupers all vere blithe and gay,
Keeping their Christmas holiday,
Vhen the master he cried with a roguish leer,
"You'll all get fat on your Christmas cheer";
And each by his looks he seem'd to say,
"I'll have some more soup on this Christmas day."

At length all of us to bed vos sent,
The boy vos missing, in search ve vent;
Ve sought him above, ve sought him below,
Ve sought him vith faces of grief and voe.
Ve sought him that hour, ve sought him that night,
Ve sought him in fear, and ve sought him in fright.
When a young pauper cried, "I knows ve shall
Get jolly vell vopt for losing our pal."

At length the soup-copper repairs did need,
The coppersmith came—and there he seed
A dollop of bones lay grizzling there,
In the leg of the breeches the boy did vear.
To gain his fill the boy did stoop,
And, dreadful to tell, he vos boiled in the soup.
And ve all of us say it, and say it vith sneers,
That he vos pushed in by the overseers.

Murder by
Fire-arm and Knife

So far as immortality is concerned, John Thurtell was more fortunate than the majority of murderers, whose main, and usually only, link with the future is by the deadline-conscious words of unbylined crime reporters. Thurtell's deed was chronicled by George Borrow[1] and Pierce Egan, both of whom knew him, and by William Hazlitt, who had once travelled in a coach with him; Thomas Carlyle, too, by quoting a witness's definition of respectability—"he kept a gig"—helped to ensure Thurtell's posterity.

The victim of the excessively brutal crime was William Weare, a card-sharper and billiards-player who had cheated Thurtell of some hundreds of pounds. In October 1823, Thurtell, who had lost heavily at other "sporting ventures" and was facing imminent prosecution for fire-raising, was desperately in need of money. Learning that Weare had backed several winners at Doncaster Races, he invited him down to Elstree for some shooting:

> 'Twas on a bright October night,
> The moon was shining clear,
> When Thurtell he set off from town,
> Accompanied by Weare.
>
> When they reached Gill's Hill Lane,
> That dark and dismal place,
> Thurtell drew a pistol forth,
> And fir'd it in Weare's face.
>
> The helpless man sprang from the gig,
> And strove the road to gain,

But Thurtell pounced on him and dash'd
His pistol through his brains.

Then drawing forth his murderous knife,
As over him he stood,
He cut his throat, and, tiger-like,
Did drink his reeking blood.[2]

Another broadsheet ballad—this one composed by William
Webb, acrobat, linkboy, and afterwards transported convict—
contained a stanza that delighted Sir Walter Scott:[3]

His throat they cut from ear to ear,
His brains they battered in;
His name was Mr. William Weare,
Wot dwelt in Lyon's Inn.

The plural form in this verse is inaccurate. Thurtell had
two accomplices—Joseph Hunt, an effeminate singer, and a
thief and general ne'er-do-well called William Probert—but
neither was present when Weare was killed. All three men
were arrested a few days after the murder. Probert hurriedly
turned king's evidence (he was hanged a year later for horse-
stealing). Despite Thurtell's long and impassioned speech,
ending with a plea not to upset his parents by having him
hanged, the jury found him guilty and he was executed out-
side Hertford Prison in January 1824. (It is recorded that his
neck, as it broke, "cracked like the shot of a pistol.") Hunt was
reprieved at the last moment and transported to Botany Bay,
where he lived for many years at Bathurst.[4]

NOTES

1. Borrow's description of Thurtell: "He was a man somewhat under
thirty and nearly six feet high. He wore neither whiskers nor moustache, and
appeared not to delight in hair, that of his head, which was of a light brown,
being closely cropped; the forehead was rather high, but somewhat narrow;
the face was neither broad nor sharp, perhaps rather sharp than broad; the
nose was almost delicate; the eyes were grey with an expression in which

there was sternness blended with something approaching to feline; his complexion was exceedingly pale, relieved, however, by certain pockmarks, which here and there studded his countenance; his form was athletic, but lean; his arms long. In the whole appearance of the man there was a blending of the bluff and the sharp. You might have supposed him a bruiser; something, however, was wanting in his manner—the quietness of the professional man; he rather looked like one performing the part—well, very well—but still performing a part."

2. There is no evidence of vampirism. What happened, it seems, is that blood gushed from the arterial wound into Thurtell's mouth, which happened to be gaping at the time.

3. Four years after the crime, when driving from London to Scotland, Scott made a diversion to Elstree to see Probert's cottage (by then half-destroyed by souvenir-hunters) and the pond in which Weare's body had been thrown. "The fatal pond is now only a green swamp," he wrote, "so near the house that one cannot conceive how it was ever chosen as a place of temporary concealment for the murdered body. Indeed, the whole history of the murder and the scenes which ensued are strange pictures of desperate and short-sighted wickedness."

4. For a full account, see *The Thurtell-Hunt Murder Case: Dark Mirror to Regency England* by Albert Borowitz, Louisiana State University Press, 1987.

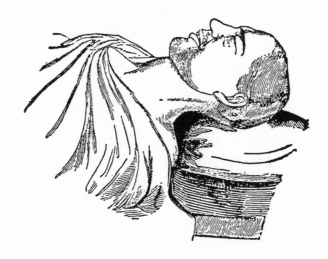

The corpse of John Thurtell

Murder by Fire-arm / 1

Maria Marten, a mole-catcher's daughter, was last seen alive on Friday, 18 May 1827, shortly before she met her lover, William Corder, in the Red Barn at Polstead, Suffolk. Corder gave several different explanations for her disappearance, telling her father that she was holidaying on the Isle of Wight, and others that she was at Yarmouth or on the Continent. Then, after borrowing £400 from his mother, Corder left for London, where he obtained a wife through an advertisement in the *Sunday Times* and settled down as a schoolmaster at Ealing. Meanwhile, Maria's stepmother was saying that she had had a series of dreams in which she had seen Corder shooting Maria and burying her in the Red Barn. Mr. Marten went to the barn and dug up the body. Corder was arrested; after a two-day trial, he was found guilty,[1] and was executed outside Bury St. Edmunds jail on 11 August 1828. He took a long time a-dying: eight minutes after the drop, and despite the efforts of the hangman, who suspended his weight on Corder's body, there was "a heaving of the shoulders, a slight convulsion of the frame, an indistinct groan."[2]

The case has been the subject of several melodramas and ballads. Many people will remember Tod Slaughter's portrayal of William Corder in *Maria Marten, or Murder in the Red Barn*, which was part of his repertoire for nearly forty years. One of the first of the ballads—if not *the* first—was sold and sung at the Polstead Cherry Fair, weeks before the trial:

Come all you thoughtless young men, a warning take by me,
And think upon my unhappy fate to be hanged upon a tree;
My name is William Corder, to you, I do declare,
I courted Maria Marten, most beautiful and fair.
I promised I would marry her upon a certain day,

THEATRE, LINCOLN.

BY DESIRE OF

G. E. WELBY, Esq. M.P. & C. FURNOR, Esq.

THE STEWARDS OF THE STUFF BALL.

On *WEDNESDAY Evening, OCTOBER 27th, 1830,*

Will be presented, the celebrated drama of

Sweethearts and Wives.

Admiral Franklin, ... Mr. SHIELD.   Charles Franklin, ... Mr. SIMMS.
Sandford, ... Mr. CULLENFORD   Curtis, ... Mr. HODGSON.
Billy Lackaday, ... Mr. GURNER.
Mrs. Bell, ... Mrs. DANBY.   Susan, ... Mrs. GURNER.
Eugenia, ... Mrs. W. ROBERTSON.   Laura, ... Miss STEWART SMITH.

A COMIC SONG ...... by ...... Mr. HODGSON.

With (for the **LAST TIME**,) the new Tragic Melo Drama, in 4 Acts, founded on Fact, called the

RED BARN;

OR, THE PROPHETIC DREAM.

THE MUSIC SELECTED AND ARRANGED BY MR. STANNARD

WITH NEW SCENERY PAINTED FOR THE OCCASION BY MR. SIMMS.

Mr. ROBERTSON is induced to bring forward this piece, not only from the unprecedented success it has been received with at the various Theatres in the Kingdom, but as a moral lesson, that Murder, however for the time concealed, will speak with most miraculous organ. Every one must be aware of the Incidents on which the Piece is founded, but the Dramatist has avoided the real names of the parties, still blending all the principal Incidents, with an effect at once awful and instructive.

Cordel, a young Farmer, ... Mr. HAMILTON.
Mr. Delamere, a Magistrate, ... Mr. BRUNTON.
Wilton, a Gipsy Confederate of Cordel, ... Mr. TALBOT.
Marlin, a labouring Farmer in the vale of years, ... Mr. STYLES.
Robin, a Factotum to Chatteral, ... Mr. SIMMS.
Peter Christopher Chatteral, a Barber, Beadle, &c. .... Mr. GURNER.
Nell Hatfield, a Gipsy, .. Mrs. W. ROBERTSON.   Anna Hatfield, her daughter, .. Mrs. GURNER.
Dame Marlin, ... Mrs. DANBY.   Mrs Cordel, ... Mrs. HAMILTON.
Maria Marlin, ... Miss STEWART SMITH.

A Brief Sketch of the Incidents:
CORDEL for his numerous Crimes receives the CURSE of the GIPSY CHIEF.

CORDEL'S FIRST MEETING WITH MARIA MARLIN.

His promise to marry her—The anguish of old Marlin and his Dame at parting with her—His proposition to meet her at the RED BARN disguised in Man's Apparel—Her joy at the thoughts of Marriage.

AWFUL MEETING AT THE RED BARN,
WHERE THE DEED IS PERPETRATED.

THE APPEARANCE OF MARIA TO HER MOTHER IN A DREAM.

𝕿𝖍𝖊 𝕴𝖓𝖙𝖊𝖗𝖎𝖔𝖗 𝖔𝖋 𝖙𝖍𝖊 𝕭𝖆𝖗𝖓 𝖜𝖍𝖊𝖗𝖊 𝖙𝖍𝖊 𝕭𝖔𝖉𝖞 𝖎𝖘 𝖉𝖎𝖘𝖈𝖔𝖛𝖊𝖗𝖊𝖉.

CORDEL's Marriage in London.—His living in splendour when the GIPSY's CURSE is fulfilled.
CORDEL'S APPREHENSION AND CONFESSION,
And the appearance of the Shade of Maria Marlin in Cordel's Dream, which produces the denouement.

Among the minor Incidents to give effect to the serious part of the Melo-drama, some Comic Parts are introduced which must set gravity at defiance.

Instead of that I was resolved to take her life away.
I went into her father's house the 18th day of May,
Saying, "My dear Maria, we will fix the wedding day.
If you will meet me at the Red Barn, as sure as I have life,
I will take you to Ipswich town, and there make you my wife."

I then went home and fetched my gun, my pickaxe and my
    spade,
I went into the Red Barn and there I dug her grave.
With heart so light, she thought no harm to meet me she did
    go,
I murdered her all in the Barn and laid her body low;
After the horrid deed was done, she lay weltering in her gore,
Her bleeding, mangled body I buried under the Red Barn
    floor.
Now all things being silent, her spirit could not rest,
She appeared unto her mother, who suckled her at her
    breast;[3]
For many a long month or more, her mind being sore op-
    press'd,
Neither night nor day she could not take any rest.
Her mother's mind, being so disturbed, she dreamt three
    nights o'er,
Her daughter she lay murdered beneath the Red Barn floor;
She sent the father to the barn when he the ground did
    thrust,
And there he found his daughter mingling with the dust.
My trial is hard, I could not stand, most woeful was the sight,
When her jaw-bone was brought to prove which pierced my
    heart quite;
Her aged father standing by, likewise his loving wife,
And in her grief her hair she tore, she scarcely could keep life.
Adieu, adieu, my loving friends, my glass is almost run,
On Monday next will be my last, when I am to be hang'd;
So you young men who do pass by, with pity look on me,
For murdering Maria Marten I was hanged upon the tree.

NOTES

1. Donald McCormick (*The Red Barn Mystery*, John Long, 1967) has res-
urrected some interesting, but mainly hearsay, information which suggests,

among other things, that while Corder was responsible for shooting Maria Marten and critically wounding her, and for burying the body, a Polstead pig-thief named "Beauty" Smith executed the *coup de grâce* when Corder was fetching a pickaxe and shovel.

Corder had a casual friendship with Thomas Griffiths Wainewright (1794–1852), minor poet and probable mass-murderer, who is the subject of Wilde's "Pen, Pencil, and Poison" (which can be found in, among other books, my anthology, *The Art of Murder,* Piatkus, 1990), and the hero of Dickens's *Hunted Down.* Wainewright afterwards wrote of Corder: "He was obviously, in retrospect, a far more complex and interesting character than I gave him credit for. He showed a genuine fondness for the truly beautiful, a surprising and rather gratifying whim in a Suffolk Satyr, and this eye for beauty was as keen in assessing the virtues of good painting as in judging feminine charms. I find it hard to believe he was a cold and calculating murderer. It would have surprised me much less to have learned that some woman had actually killed him. He had a capacity for thinking for himself, for dreaming of Elysian fields and the knelling horn of Aurora's love, and of wanting to escape from the horrors of a routine life among the pigs. Why, when he was not making love to some rustic beauty, he was actually contemplating the religious life. A passing phase of youth perhaps, but true nonetheless. He was far too much a dreamer ever to make a murderer, much less a successful one. But no doubt the Law demanded a victim and Corder was ready-made for the part."

2. The next day the body was taken to the West Suffolk General Hospital for dissection. The skeleton was exhibited publicly at the hospital for some time, and the following account appeared in a local newspaper in 1841: "The skeleton of Corder, the murderer, has been placed in a recess of the museum of the Suffolk Infirmary, Bury St. Edmunds. It is covered with a glass case, beneath which is a box for contributions. Every visitor is expected to put silver into this box, which money is applied to the wants of the necessitous patients. By an ingeniously constructed spring, the arm of the skeleton points towards the box as soon as the visitors approach it. The receipts are said to average £50 per annum. (The ingenuity seems to us to be much misapplied. There are few females who would not be terrified at such an exhibition and in some cases it might produce very serious consequences.)" Corder's skeleton is now in the Museum of the Royal College of Surgeons of England, which also houses the skeletal remains of, among other criminals, John Thurtell; Eugene Aram, who was executed in 1759 for a murder committed fourteen years before (Thomas Hood's "The Dream of Eugene Aram" is too long for inclusion in this collection); and Jonathan Wild, the Thief-Taker General, who in 1724, at the Old Bailey, had his throat slit, not lethally, by a highwayman known as Blueskin whom he had framed (the incident inspired Dean Swift to write an elegy, "Blueskin's Ballad"), and who was himself hanged— for procuring the return of stolen lace—in the following year.

3. A mistake. It was the stepmother who, so she said, had the dream.

Murder by Fire-arm / 2

Charles Guiteau, a paranoid swindler and fringe-religionist who was barely five feet tall, shot President James A. Garfield on 2 July 1881. The motive, it seems, was disappointment:[1] during the presidential campaign, Guiteau had written a pamphlet in support of Garfield, and when the ungrateful president offered him neither the Austrian ambassadorship nor the Paris consulship, Guiteau, his disappointment increased by the belief that Garfield was betraying his party, bought a revolver and shot him as he was walking to board a train at the Baltimore & Potomac Depot in Washington. Guiteau was arrested immediately. The president, still alive, was taken back to the White House, and was later moved to his seaside cottage at Elberon, New Jersey, where he died on 19 September. The *New York Tribune* epitomized the general attitude to Guiteau in a poem published the day after Garfield's death:

> That life so mean should murder life so great!
> What is there left to us who think and feel,
> Who have no remedy and no appeal,
> But damn the wasp and crush him under heel?

Annemarie Ewing and Morris Bishop[2] say that the following verses are "alleged to be the work of the murderer Guiteau himself, who supposedly sang them proudly to visitors in his cell":

> Come all you tender Christians,
> Wherever you may be,
> And likewise pay attention

FRANK LESLIE'S
ILLUSTRATED
NEWSPAPER

Entered according to Act of Congress, in the year 1882, by Mrs. FRANK LESLIE, in the Office of the Librarian of Congress at Washington.— Entered at the Post Office, New York, N.Y., as Second-class Matter.

No. 1,398.—Vol. LIV.　　　NEW YORK—FOR THE WEEK ENDING JULY 8, 1882.　　　[PRICE 10 CENTS.　$4.00 YEARLY, 10 WEEKS, $1.00.

WASHINGTON, D. C.—THE CLOSING ACT IN THE GREAT NATIONAL TRAGEDY.—MEDICAL EXAMINATION OF GUITEAU'S BODY AFTER THE EXECUTION.—FROM A SKETCH BY C. B. BUNNELL.—SEE PAGE 311.

To these few lines you see.
For the murder of James A. Garfield
I am condemned to die,
On the thirtieth day of June,
Upon the scaffold high.

My name is Charles Guiteau,
My name I'll never deny,
I left my aged parents
In sorrow for to die,
But little did they think
When in my youthful bloom,
I'd ever climb the gallows high
To meet my fatal doom.

'Twas down by the depot
I tried to make my escape,
But providence was against me
And I found it was too late.
I tried to plead insane
But found it would not go;
The people was all against me
And I did not get no show.

My sister came to see me
To bid her last farewell;
She threw her arms around my neck
And wept most bitterly.
She says, My darling brother,
You're surely going to die,
On the thirtieth day of June,
Upon the scaffold high.

At noon on 30 June 1882, after a lavish meal, Guiteau
mounted the scaffold and, with a clergyman acting as lectern
for a Bible, read aloud fourteen verses from Matthew 10,
starting with the words, "And fear not them that kill the body
but are not able to kill the soul." He then told the assembled
reporters: "I am now going to read some verses which are in-
tended to indicate my feelings at the moment of leaving this

world. If set to music, they may be rendered very effective.
The idea is that of a child babbling to his mama and his papa.
I wrote it this morning about ten o'clock."

Guiteau proceeded to recite in a high-pitched voice:

> I am going to the Lordy, I am so glad,
> I am going to the Lordy, I am so glad,
>   I am going to the Lordy,
> Glory hallelujah! Glory hallelujah!
>   I am going to the Lordy.
> I love the Lordy with all my soul,
>   Glory hallelujah!
> And that is the reason I am going to the Lord,
> Glory hallelujah! Glory hallelujah!
>   I am going to the Lord.
> I saved my party and my land,
>   Glory hallelujah!
> But they have murdered me for it,
> And that is the reason I am going to the Lordy,
> Glory hallelujah! Glory hallelujah!
>   I am going to the Lordy!
> I wonder what I will do when I get to the Lordy,
> I guess that I will weep no more
> When I get to the Lordy!
>   Glory hallelujah!
> I wonder what I will see when I get to the Lordy,
> I expect to see most glorious things,
> Beyond all earthly conception,
> When I am with the Lordy!
> Glory hallelujah! Glory hallelujah!
>   I am with the Lord.

The black cap was placed over Guiteau's face. He dropped the manuscript. "Glory, ready, go," he said loudly, and the hangman pulled the lever.

NOTES

1. According to Miss F. Tennyson Jesse (*Murder and Its Motives*, Harrap, 1924 and 1952), "Every murder falls into one of six classes. . . . I. Murder for

gain. II. Murder for revenge. III. Murder for elimination. IV. Murder for jealousy. V. Murder for the lust of killing. VI. Murder from conviction." Few people would argue with this classification; even so, it is hard to say in which class Guiteau's crime should be placed.

2. In *The New Yorker*, 18 March 1939.

Murder by Fire-arm / 3

According to a collector of "Frankie and Albert (or Johnny)" songs, there are more than a hundred versions of the lyric.[1] The origin of the protean lyric-tale is subject to debate. Some say that it refers to the shooting of Allen Britt, an eighteen-year-old black man, by Frankie Baker, a mulatto woman with whom he was living, in St. Louis, Missouri, on 15 October 1899; Britt died four days later. Frankie Baker testified that he threatened her with a knife and that she fired at him in self-defense. In 1939, Miss Baker, "the proprietor of a shoe-shine place," brought an action for two hundred thousand dollars in damages against Republic Pictures for allegedly defaming her character and invading her privacy in a film based on the song. During the case, which was eventually dismissed in 1942, she claimed that there were no "Frankie and Johnny" songs until after she killed Britt. There appears to be evidence, however, that the song has a longer history: Orrick Johns[2] claims that it originated with Mammy Lou, "a blues singer at Babe Connors's bawdy-house in St. Louis," in the early 1890s, and that Mammy Lou sang it for Paderewski; another theory is that Frankie was Frankie Silver, a white woman who murdered her husband at Toe River, North Carolina, as far back as 1831.[3] But everyone seems to agree that Albert was rechristened Johnny by the Leighton Brothers, a music hall act, in 1911. This is one of the pre-Johnny versions:

> Frankie was a good girl,
> Everybody knows,
> She paid half a hundred
> For Albert a suit of clothes,
> He is my man, but he won't come home.

Way down in some dark alley
I heard a bulldog bark,
I believe to my soul my honey
Is lost out in the dark,
He is my man, but he won't come home.

Frankie went uptown this morning,
She did not go for fun,
Under her apron she carried
Albert's forty-one,
He is my man, but he won't come home.

Frankie went to the bartender,
Called for a bottle of beer
Asked him, my loving Albert,
Has he been here?
He is my man, but he won't come home.

Bartender said to Frankie,
I can't tell you a lie,
He left here about an hour ago
With a girl called Alice Bly,
He is your man, but he's doing you wrong.

Frankie went up Fourth Street,
Come back down on Main,
Looking up on the second floor,
Saw Albert in another girl's arms,
Saying he's my man, but he's doing me wrong.

Frankie says to Albert,
Baby, don't you run!
If you don't come to the one you love
I'll shoot you with your own gun,
You are my man, but you're doing me wrong.

Frankie, she shot Albert,
He fell upon the floor,
Says, turn me over easy,
And turn me over slow,
I'm your man, but you shot me down.

versicles

43

Early the next morning,
Just about half-past four,
Eighteen inches of black crêpe
Was hanging on Frankie's door,
Saying he was my man, but he wouldn't come home.

Frankie went over to Mis' Moodie's,
Fell upon her knees,
Says, forgive me, Mis' Moodie,
Forgive me, oh do, please.
How can I when he's my only son?

Frankie went down to the graveyard,
Police by her side,
When she saw the one she loved,
She hollered and she cried,
He was my man, but he wouldn't come home.

Police said to Frankie,
No use to holler and cry,
When you shot the one you loved,
You meant for him to die,
He's your man, but he's dead and gone.

Rubber-tyred buggy,
Silver-mounted hack,
Took Albert to the graveyard
But couldn't bring him back,
He was my man, but he wouldn't come home.

NOTES

1. George Milburn quoted in *Ozark Folk Songs*, edited by Vance Randolph, The State Historical Society of Missouri, 1948.
2. *The Time of Our Lives*, Stackpole, 1937.
3. *Bulletin of the Folk-Song Society of the Northeast*, no. 10, 1935. (There is a "Frankie Silver" ballad, but it is not included in this collection.)

Murder by Fire-arm / 4

This ballad is said to refer to a murder that occurred about 1900 at Grandin, Missouri.

The Murder of Charley Stacey

Come all you young people and listen while I tell
A story that was told me long ago,
About a tragic murder that happened near the spring
Where Little Black River's waters calmly flow.

It occurred one Sabbath morning, the birds were singing gay,
And everyone was happy as could be;
Poor Charley never thought that morn that ere the sun went down,
He would sleep so silent underneath the lea.

The fatal mob was drunk that night, they numbered three in all,
And one of them was hating Charley's heart,
Because he'd won the virtuous love of a native maiden fair,
From which he vowed that he would never part.

They gathered round Black River spring to wait the boy's return,
For Charley and his sweetheart were at church.
When they saw him coming, they assumed a dreadful frown
And from their lips came deadly peals of curses.

They quickly drew their pistols, we heard the loud reports,
Poor Charley fell, then staggered to his knees.
He swiftly drew his weapon, and one of them dropped down,
While the white smoke floated on the spring-time breeze.

44

He's sleeping in the churchyard fair, where sunny violets
    bloom,
Where the wild rose creeps so silent o'er his grave.
I believe that God in Heaven will open wide the door
And bid poor Charley Stacey enter in.

bloody

versicles

45

Murder by Fire-arm / 5

On the night of Sunday, 2 November 1952, the police were called to investigate a break-in at a confectionery warehouse in Croydon, Surrey. During a fracas on the roof of the building, one of the intruders, nineteen-year-old Derek Bentley, was taken into custody. But the other intruder, sixteen-year-old Christopher Craig (whose older brother had three days before been sentenced to twelve years' imprisonment for armed robbery), produced a revolver and held the police at bay. Bentley shouted, "Let them have it, Chris" (an ambiguous remark; but, according to police testimony, Bentley certainly did not mean that Craig should hand over the gun). Craig fired at Detective Constable Fairfax, who was holding Bentley, and wounded him in the shoulder. He then shot Police Constable Miles between the eyes. Later, after firearms had been brought for the police, Craig jumped from the roof. Before losing consciousness he said, "I hope I've killed the fucking lot."

At the trial at the Old Bailey before the lord chief justice, Lord Goddard, both Craig and Bentley were found guilty of the murder of P. C. Miles. Bentley was executed at Wandsworth Prison on 28 January 1953. Craig, because of his age, was sentenced to be detained. He was released in 1968.

The chorus of the following ballad by Karl Dallas refers to the testimony of Craig's father, a bank cashier, that his son, who suffered from "word blindness," enjoyed American horror comics and films.[1] Mr. Craig, who himself owned a revolver, admitted that he had taught his sons to shoot with air guns.

Derek Bentley

It's of a great adventure to you that I will tell,
Of how they hanged a silly boy and how it all befell.
(*Chorus*) It was guns and comics, films of war, that made his
education.

Young Craig and Derek Bentley, they went out in the night
With gun and knuckleduster just for to see them right.
(*Chorus*)

They climbed upon the roof so high and then looked all
around,
And there they saw the men of law all gathered on the
ground.
(*Chorus*)

"Look out, we're caught," young Bentley cried, "our robbing
days are done."
"I'll see no prison," Craig replied, "while I've still got my
gun."
(*Chorus*)

He stood upon the roof so high, and he looked all around,
And shouted to the men of law all gathered on the ground.
(*Chorus*)

"Stay down and stay alive," he cried. "Keep clear of me," he
said,
"Come up that stair another step and you'll go down it dead."
(*Chorus*)

He was just a silly frightened boy who couldn't read or write,
But standing there with gun in hand, he terrorized the night.
(*Chorus*)

The men came up to take him down; he pressed the trigger
tight;
He shot the first one dead and then jumped down into the
night.
(*Chorus*)

Now Craig, he was a killer, for he shot the policeman dead,
But they couldn't hang a boy so young, the magistrates they
said.
(*Chorus*)

At nine o'clock one Wednesday, they took young Bentley out,
And made a noose of hempen rope and put it round his
throat.
(*Chorus*)

It's true, as you have often heard, that in this land today,
They hang the little criminals and let the big go free.
(*Chorus*)

NOTE

1. Craig himself testified that he went to the cinema three or four times a
week and that his preference was for gangster films. In his Introduction to
Trial of Craig and Bentley (Hodge, 1954), H. Mongomery Hyde writes: "On
the very afternoon of the crime he [Craig] had been to see *My Death is a Mock-
ery*, a film in which the hero is hanged as the result of a fight in which a
French policeman is shot." According to Craig's father, "the only books he
knew anything about were the books of Enid Blyton that he got other people
to read to him."

Murder by Fire-arm / 6

On Monday, 10 March 1980, Mrs. Jean Harris, a fifty-six-year-old divorcée, drove the five hundred miles from the posh Madeira School at McLean, Virginia, at which she was headmistress, to Scarsdale, New York, to the mansion of Dr. Herman Tarnower. The doctor had made, and was still making, fat profits from a diet plan that he had concocted. He had also been Mrs. Harris's lover—until recently, that is, when she had been supplanted by a younger woman. By the time Mrs. Harris, who had not told the doctor to expect her, arrived, he was in bed, alone. To cut short the long story that she told the police soon afterwards, Tarnower grumbled at being awoken, and there was a fierce argument, which was terminated when she, having taken a .32-caliber revolver from her purse, shot the doctor four times. He soon bled to death. She claimed that she had intended to kill herself and that he had jogged her arm. The police didn't believe her story; nor did the jury at her trial. (When Ellen Burstyn played Mrs. Harris in a television reconstruction of the trial, she made the story sound far more likely.) Found guilty of murder in the second degree, Mrs. Harris was sentenced to imprisonment for fifteen years to life.

The press made much of the case—and almost as much of things that had nothing to do with it. Mrs. Thomas M. (Bea) McDade, living in Purchase, a town close to Scarsdale, was called upon by a reporter, accompanied by a photographer who took a snap of her; the next day a report was illustrated with the picture, captioned: "This neighbor of the dead diet doctor says she cannot remember ever seeing him." Newspaper reports revealed that Mrs. Harris had been living a double life. While keeping her love affair secret, the headmistress was a matchless martinet at Madeira: upset by the sight of orange peel littering the well-tailored lawns, she banned the eating of citrus fruit on the campus.[1]

To change the subject: Albert Borowitz, the American crime historian and novelist, is a lawyer as well as the author of a short musical comedy, *The Trial of Mrs. H.*, which was first performed at Cleveland, Ohio, in 1981. Each of the show's numbers uses the music of a classic popular song. For instance, "Madeira" (sung by a reincarnated Lizzie Borden, who, called as a character-witness for the defendant, has just said of her: "When she herself was at school, she was voted most likely to succeed . . . by the rifle team. And the same great team-spirit prevails at Madeira") is set to the tune of "Maria," from *West Side Story:*

> Madeira—she taught at a school named Madeira,
> Where everyone's the same,
> With just as perfect aim as she.
>
> Madeira! Let's put in a plug for Madeira:
> The campus is a beaut,
> No rinds of citrus fruit
> You'll see.
> Madeira!
>
> Say it soft and there's music playing,
> Say it loud and the bullets are spraying—
> Madeira. I'll never stop saying Madeira!

NOTE

1. For a long account of the case, see *Mrs. Harris: The Death of the Scarsdale Diet Doctor* by Diana Trilling (Harcourt Brace Jovanovich, 1981); for an essay on it, see Molly Tibbs's in my anthology, *The Lady Killers* (Piatkus, 1990); and for Jean Harris's own version, see her *Stranger in Two Worlds* (Macmillan, USA, 1986).

Murder by Horseshoe Rasp

The song below (to the tune of "The Boston Burglar") was written by Lloyd Robinson while he was remanded in custody at Marshfield, Missouri, for the murder of his father on 3 June 1935. At the trial, he admitted patricide, but the judge (who must have credited his claim that he had been egged on to do it by little people who had somehow gotten into his brain) sentenced him to life imprisonment rather than execution or incarceration in a lunatic asylum. Going by the last line of the song, the sentence was the one Robinson had expected—and perhaps angled for.

> They put me up to kill him,
> My pore old white-haired dad,
> I done it with a horseshoe rasp,
> The only thing I had.
>
> I snuck right up behind him,
> While he ate his supper cold,
> I hit him once upon the head,
> Just like I was told.
>
> He didn't make no holler,
> All he did was groan,
> My maw, she grabbed him by the feet
> And my, how she did moan.
>
> And now I sure am sorry
> I done this terrible crime,
> For killin' my pore old daddy
> I'll soon be doing time.

Murder by Knife / 1

The date, place, and names of the principals in this broad-sheet ballad seem to have disappeared. Buxton is in Derbyshire, not Staffordshire, and the local librarian and curator, Mr. I. E. Burton, has been unable to trace the crime in his records. Although data-less, the ballad is of interest, I think—perhaps especially to gynecologists.

The Cruel Gamekeeper

In Buxton Town in Staffordshire,
A farmer's daughter lived there;
On a gamekeeper, as we find,
This damsel she did fix her mind.

It happened lately in the Park,
She met her lover with an aching heart;
She said, "My dear, what shall I do
(For I am big with child by you)?"

"I will not marry yet," said he,
"For while I'm single I am free."
From his pocket a knife he drew
And pierced her tender body through.

He ripped her up and, by and by,
A baby in her womb did cry;
He then did hide her among some thorns,
The baby crawling in her arms.

They took the keeper before it was long
And bound him in a prison strong,
And he was soon condemned to die,
All on the gallows tree so high.

Murder by Knife / 2

In common with several of his literary contemporaries, Charles Lamb (1775–1834) took an interest in crime and punishment—particularly, and perhaps peculiarly, in the subject of survival after hanging.[1]

In January 1829, hearing of the marriage of his friend, Louisa Holcroft, to Dr. J. Badams, Lamb wrote to Bryan Waller Proctor[2] from his home on the Chase at Enfield:

> Who is Badman, or Bed'em? . . . I hear he is a great chymist. I am sometimes chymical myself. A thought strikes me with horror. Pray heaven he may not have done it for the sake of trying chymical experiments upon her,—young female subjects are so scarce! Louisa would make a capital shot.[3] An't you glad about Burke's case? We may set off the Scotch murders against the Scotch novels—Hare, the Great Un-hanged.[4]

In December 1832, Lamb's interest in crime became more than scholarly—indeed, it seems that for a short while he was actually under suspicion of being an accessory to murder.[5] On the nineteenth, a young man named Benjamin Couch Danby, who had just returned from India and was thought to have money about him, spent the evening at the Crown & Horseshoe, Enfield, in the company of William Johnson, John Cooper, and Samuel Fare. At closing time, the three men took Danby up Holt White's Hill, where they robbed and murdered him. The crime was versified in a broadsheet ballad:

> Give ear, ye tender Christians all, and listen unto me,
> While I relate a deed of blood and great barbarity;

A murder of the blackest dye I now repeat in rhyme,
Committed on Benjamin Danby, a young man in his prime.

This young man was a sailor, and just returned from sea,
And down to Enfield Chase he went, his cousin for to see,
With money in his pocket, so jolly and so free,
But little did he dream of such a dismal destiny.

'Twas on a Wednesday ev'ning he call'd at the Horseshoe,
And there he drank so freely, as sailors mostly do;
Some ruffians in the company whom he did treat most kind,
To rob and murder him that night most wickedly designed.

They threw him on the ground and then stabbed him with a
    knife;
He cried out, "Do not murder me!—O do not take my life!"
But heedless of his piteous cries, his throat they cut quite
    deep,
And turn'd the gully in his throat as butchers kill their sheep.

Then in a ditch they threw his corpse, mangled with ghastly
    wounds,
Where early the next morning the body it was found.
Now Cooper, Fare and Johnson are committed for this crime,
And will be tried at Newgate all in a little time.

Lamb explained his involvement in the case in a letter to
Louisa Badams, written on New Year's Eve, 1832:

> . . . I have been not a little disconcerted.
>   On the night of our murder (an hour or two before
> it), the maid being busy, I went out to order an addi-
> tional pint of porter for Moxon[6] who had surprised us
> with a late visit. Now I never go out quite disinterested
> upon such occasions. And I begged a half-pint of ale at
> the bar which our sweet-faced landlady good-humoredly
> complied with, asking me into the parlor, but a side door
> was just open that disclosed a more cheerful blaze, and
> I entered where four people were engaged over Domi-
> noes. One of them, Fare, invited me to join in it, partly
> out of impudence, I believe; however, not to balk a

Christmas frolic, I complied, and played with Danby, but soon gave over, having forgot the game. I was surprised with D. challenging me as having known me in the Temple. He must have been a child then. I did not recognize him, but perfectly remembered his father, who was a hairdresser in the Temple. This was all that passed, as I went away with my beer. Judge my surprise when the next morning I was summoned before Dr. Creswell to say what I knew of the transaction. My examination was conducted with all delicacy, and of course I was soon dismissed. I was afraid of getting into the papers, but I was pleased to find myself only noticed as a "gentleman whose name we could not gather."

Poor D.! The few words I spoke to him were to remind him of a trick Jem White played upon his father. The boy was too young to know anything about it. In the *Morning Post* appeared this paragraph: "Yesterday morning, Mr. Danby, the respectable Hairdresser in Pump Court in the Temple, in a fit of delirium threw himself out of a 2 pair stairs window, looking into the passage that leads to Fig-tree Court, and his head was literally smashed to atoms." White went to D.'s to see how it operated, and found D. quietly weaving wigs, and the shop full of lawyers that had come to enquire particulars. D. was a man much respected. Indeed hairdressers in the Inns of Court are a superior race of tradesmen. They generally leave off rich, as D. did.

Well, poor D. had never heard the story or probably forgotten it—and his company looked on me a little suspiciously, as they do at alehouses when a rather better drest person than themselves attempts to join 'em—(it never answers,—at least it seemed so to me when I heard of the murder)—I went away. One often fancies things afterwards that did not perhaps strike one at the time. However, after all, I have felt queer ever since. It has almost sickened me of the Crown and Horseshoe, and I sha'n't hastily go into the taproom again.

As soon as he had recovered from the "feeling of queerness," Lamb invited Moxon to Enfield, telling him that

"Johnson and Fare's sheets have been wash'd—unless you prefer Danby's *last* bed—at the Horseshoe."

At the trial at the Old Bailey in January, Cooper turned king's evidence and Fare was acquitted, but Johnson was convicted and sentenced to death. Lamb wrote to Louisa Badams on 15 February 1833:

> Thanks for your remembrance of your old fellow-prisoners at murderous Enfield. By the way, Cooper, who turned King's evidence, is come back again Whitewash'd, has resumed his seat at chapel, and took his sister (a fact!) up the Holt White's lane to shew her the topography of the deed. I intend asking him to supper. They say he's pleasant in conversation. Will you come and meet him?

NOTES

1. See his *Reflector* essay, "On the Inconveniences of Being Hanged"; also his farce, *The Pawnbroker's Daughter.*

2. A minor poet who wrote under the pen name of Barry Cornwall.

3. Burke and Hare (see page 120) referred to their homemade corpses as "shots."

4. When the Waverley novels first appeared, the anonymous author was called "the Great Unknown."

5. In 1796, Lamb's elder sister Mary, overwork and anxiety affecting her mind, had become so irritated with a young home-help that she chased the girl around the sitting room with a knife. Then, further irritated by the efforts of her own mother—an invalid, not quite right in the head—to hinder her efforts to catch the girl, she stabbed the old woman to death. Found by a coroner's jury to be temporarily insane, Mary had been put into the custody of Charles, then just of age, who had undertaken to be her guardian.

6. Edward Moxon, Lamb's friend and publisher.

Murder by Knife and Axe

In 1835, while awaiting execution for the murder of an elderly widow and her son, Pierre-François Lacenaire—man of letters, revolutionary, and criminal—wrote his memoirs[1]; these were published in a journal edited by Dostoyevski, and it has been suggested that some of the traits of both Raskolnikov and Stavrogin were borrowed from Lacenaire. He is one of the characters in Marcel Carné's film, *Les Enfants du Paradis.*[2]

The day before his execution, Lacenaire composed a poem that ended with the lines:

> Dieu que j'invoque, écoute ma prière!
> Darde en mon âme un rayon de ta foi,
> Car je rougis de n'être que matière,
> Et cependant je doute malgré moi—
> Pardonne-moi, si dans ta créature
> Mon oeil superbe a méconnu ta main.
> Dieu—le néant—notre âme—la nature,
> C'est un secret;—je le saurai demain.

A rough translation:

> Oh God, I entreat you, hear my prayer!
> Lance a ray of faith into my soul,
> For I am ashamed that I am only gross matter—
> And, in spite of myself, I am still full of doubt.
> Forgive me if your creature's
> Proud eye has denied your hand.
> God—eternity—man's soul—Nature:
> All is a secret. Tomorrow I shall know.

1. *The Memoirs of Lacenaire,* translated and edited by Philip John Stead, Staples Press, 1952.

2. An entry from *The Master Eccentric: The Journals of Rayner Heppenstall, 1969–1981* (Allison & Busby, 1986), which I edited:

26 May 1969

I saw *Les Enfants du Paradis* shortly after the War. I was principally taken, like everyone else, with the miming of Jean-Louis Barrault and an extraordinary comic performance by Pierre Brasseur. I did not then know that most of the characters were based on historical figures or that the book was by Jacques Prévert. I did not know this for some years after meeting both Prévert and the actor, Marcel Herrand, who had played the murderer Lacenaire, of whom at the time I had never heard, but with whom I am now much concerned [for Lacenaire was one of the main figures in Heppenstall's work in progress, *French Crime in the Romantic Age,* published by Hamish Hamilton in 1970]. I have been watching for a repeat showing of the film and noticed only this morning that it was on at the Academy cinema today, Whit Monday. M. [Margaret, Heppenstall's wife] and I went to see it this afternoon. Less good in a number of ways than it seemed when I first saw it, but still very nice.

Murder by Knife / 3

Has anyone seen him? Can you tell us where he is?
If you meet him you must take away his knife.
Then give him to the ladies. They'll spoil his pretty fizz,
And I wouldn't give you tuppence for his life.

From a broadsheet,
September 1888

Jack the Ripper has been credited—if that is the word—with
as many as eleven murders in the Whitechapel area, but it is
now generally reckoned that his actual tally of "women of the
unfortunate class" was five:

Mary Ann Nicholls, Friday, 31 August 1888
Annie Chapman, Saturday, 8 September 1888
Elizabeth Stride and Catherine Eddowes,
    Sunday, 30 September 1888
Mary Jane Kelly, Friday, 9 November 1888

Although he certainly cannot have believed that the pen is
mightier than the sword, he seems to have been as prolific as
a letter writer as he was extravagant as a murderer. Dr.
Thomas Dutton, a friend of the rippings-investigating Chief
Inspector Abberline and a student of microphotography, ex-
amined 128 letters and postcards purporting to come from
the killer himself, and concluded that at least 34 were genu-
ine. The correspondence was addressed to the Central Press
Agency, to the police, and to individuals. (George Lusk, a
member of the Whitechapel Vigilance Committee, received a
"ginny" kidney by parcel post; with it was a note that read:

The Globe

SATURDAY — FEB. 14

SPECIAL EDITION

THE
MURDERS
THE POLICE BELIEVE
"JACK" CAUGHT
SPECIAL DETAILS
INQUEST TO-DAY
TO-DAY'S FOOTBALL

"Mr. Lusk, sir, I send you half the kidne I took from one woman, prasarved it to you, tother piece I fried and ate it; was very nice.") Not all of the correspondence was in prose:

Eight little whores, with no hope of heaven,
Gladstone may save one, then there'll be seven.
Seven little whores begging for a shilling,
One stays in Henege Court, then there's a killing.

Six little whores, glad to be alive,
One sidles up to Jack, then there are five.
Four and whore rhyme aright, so do three and me.
I'll set the town alight, ere there are two.

Two little whores, shivering with fright,
Seek a cozy doorway, in the middle of the night.
Jack's knife flashes, then there's but one.
And the last one's the ripest for Jack's idea of fun.

☞

Up and down the goddam town
Policemen try to find me.
But I ain't a chap yet to drown
in drink, or Thames or sea.

☞

I've no time to tell you how
I came to be a killer.
But you should know, as time will show,
that I'm society's pillar.

☞

I'm not a butcher,
I'm not a Yid,
Nor yet a foreign skipper,

But I'm your own light-hearted friend,
Yours truly, Jack the Ripper.

Many theories have been put forward as to the identity of Jack the Ripper,[1] but none succeeds in fitting all the facts. Many suggestions have been made as to what happened to him after he had distributed Mary Kelly's body about the room in Miller's Court; some are more likely than others, but all are as open to argument as the chant which children still skip to in the East End streets:

> Jack the Ripper's dead,
> And lying on his bed.
> He cut his throat
> With Sunlight Soap.
> Jack the Ripper's dead.

NOTE

1. Including: Joseph Barnett, a porter at Billingsgate fish market who at one time lived with Mary Jane Kelly; Prince Albert Victor, Duke of Clarence; Dr. Thomas Neill Cream—or a doppel-gänger, since Cream appears to have been in an American prison when the murders were committed; Frederick Bailey Deeming (see page 13)—suspected simply because he, like Dr. Cream, is said to have waited until the noose was adjusted before starting to brag that he was the Ripper, only to have the pretentious sentence curtailed by the legal one; Montague John Druitt, a cricket-playing lawyer turned schoolmaster who committed suicide a month or so after the murder of Mary Jane Kelly; Sir William Withey Gull, physician in ordinary to Queen Victoria, and accomplices in the persons of Sir Robert Anderson, the head of the Criminal Investigation Department of the Metropolitan Police, and John Netley, who had been the Duke of Clarence's carriage driver; "Jill the Ripper," a psychopathic midwife; Severin Klosowski, otherwise known as George Chapman, an innkeeper who was hanged for triple-murder by poisoning in 1903; Alexander Pedachenko, also known as Vassily Konovalov, Andrey Luiskovo, and Mikhail Ostrong (or Ostrog), an insane Russian doctor working for the Okhrana, the Tsarist secret police; Jack Pizer, or Kosminski ("Leather Apron"), an insane Polish Jew; an unnamed secretary of General William Booth, founder of the Salvation Army; an unnamed man, employed to slaughter animals by the Jewish ritual method; "Dr. Stanley," a Harley Street surgeon; James Kenneth Stephen, a writer of parodies and doggerel, and, incidentally, a relative of both Virginia Woolf and Mr. Justice Stephen (see page 86).

In a book called *Who He?* (1984), which the excellent publishers, Buchan & Enright, subtitled *Goodman's Dictionary of the Unknown Famous*, I included a spoof entry for the "real" Jack the Ripper:

Harpick, Peter J.
A transvestite sculptor, innovative in his use of Plasticine, whose mother Adascha Harpick, *née* Schmidt, was a keen cricketer (collections of sports statistics, though not *Wisden*, record that she scored a half-century on behalf of a Women of Kent XI during a friendly match with the Ladies of South Kensington at Fontwell Park in 1860) and whose father Wally is said to have been descended from the Romanovs by way of a Brighton peer. In early manhood, after studying under Dr. Wilhelm Bunbury at the Chorlton-cum-Hardy Polytechnic, Harpick developed an obsession that his mother was a surrogate, standing in, as it were, for a woman of Whitechapel's unfortunate class who had actually borne him. In the autumn of 1888, he determined to put an end to all prostitutes in that area, and, being methodical, started off with those who were unfortunate enough to have an "a" in their names. After doing away with a half a dozen, between times writing provocatively to the press, signing the messages with an anagram of his name, he became bored with the whole idea, and retired to southeast London, where he died in obscurity soon after publishing his monumental work, *Statues to be Observed in Penge and Its Environs: a Rambler's Guide* (1903), which was dedicated to "my only true begetter, Mr. W. H." (his late father, of course).

I meant that to poke fun at the "Hunt the Ripper" game: I assumed that all readers would understand that the name of my "candidate" was an anagram of the alias, that the potted biography was a fiction—therefore, I was surprised to receive a letter from a Ripperologist, requesting further information about Peter J. Harpick, and I remain astonished that a dozen other people subsequently wrote me similar letters. I must say, I found it rather hard to compose polite replies. The fact that I, not intending to fool a single reader, fooled a number of them just goes to show how easy it is for Ripper writers who aim to deceive readers into accepting their particular candidates to achieve partial success: the simple trick is to put forward a few biographical truths that do not conflict with the notion that the candidate fills the bill, add some assumptions in the guise of truths, and omit—or think up a way of discounting—proof that the theory is nutty.

Early in 1988, the Ripper Centenary Year, the *Daily Telegraph* gave considerable publicity to a new hair-brained assertion that Jack had been identified. The paper published a letter of mine to the editor, pointing out objections to the theory, and ending: "Let us agree that Jack the Ripper was Peter J. Harpick and leave him at that." And again I received tell-us-more-about-Harpick mail.

Later in the year, when the Centenary Celebrations were in full swing, I wrote "Whitechapel Blues," which was first published in the monthly *True Detective:*

A hundred years since Ripping Jack—
Forgive me if I don't look back;

I'm tired of Clarence, Chapman, Druitt—
None of them had the nous to do it.
Another thing: we can't be sure
If there was one Jack, two, or more:
Copy-cat killings have been known
To be ascribed to one alone.
There's all the talk of "Jill" as well—
Lily Langtry, Ethel M. Dell:
Maybe it *was* a fatal femme,
But frankly, I don't give a damn.
So far as I'm concerned, the rippin'
May all have been done by Dr. Crippen.
I know he wasn't even here; he
Was in the States. It's just a theory—
Along the lines of those I've heard
From Ripper buffs, and quite as absurd.
There you observe my boredom's root:
Hunt the Ripper is a trivialized pursuit.

Murder by Knife / 4

The murder of Hiram Sawtell by his brother Isaac, which occurred in New Hampshire in the early 1890s, inspired the couplet:

> Two brothers in our town did dwell;
> Hiram sought Heaven, but Isaac Sawtell.

Murder by Knife / 5

In 1896, the decapitated body of a young woman wearing a graduation dress was found at Fort Thomas, Kentucky, across the Ohio River from Cincinnati. The postmortem examination showed that she was in the family way. Her shoes had been bought at a store in Greencastle, Indiana, and their small size jogged the memory of an assistant, who recalled that they had been bought by a local girl named Pearl Bryan. It was learned that she had gone to visit her beau, a personable young man named Scott Jackson who was studying dentistry in Cincinnati, and the police soon collected enough evidence to justify his arrest, the likely motive for the murder being his desire to remain a bachelor. Arrested with Jackson was a fellow student, Alonzo Walling, against whom the evidence was far from conclusive. Both were found guilty, and, despite a good deal of public disquiet about the verdict in Walling's case, both were hanged on 20 March 1897. Pearl Bryan's head (like Belle Elmore's) was never found.

The best-known ballad on the case ends with the stanza:

> Pearl Bryan left her parents
> On a dark and gloomy day.
> She went to meet the villain
> In a spot not far away.
> She thought it was the lover's hand
> That she could trust each day.
> Alas! it was a lover's hand
> That took her life away.

There are several more Pearl Bryan ballads, most of them romanticizing the story and perverting the facts, and the following is representative:

Last night as the moon was shinin',
An' the stars was shinin' too,
Up to her cottage window
Scott Jackson, her lover, drew.

Dear Pearly, let's take a ramble
Out over the meadows gay,
There is no one to disturb us,
We will name our weddin' day.

Scott Jackson, I am so weary
That I do not care to roam,
For roamin' is so dreary,
I pray you take me home.

Down in this valley I have you,
From me you cannot fly,
No human hand can save you,
In a moment you must die.

What have I done, Scott Jackson,
That you should take my life?
You know I've always loved you,
An' would have been your wife.

Down on her knees before him,
She was prayin' to God for her life,
When into her snowy white bosum
He plunged the fatal knife.

There's room for your picture in my album,
There's room for my love in your heart,
There's room for us both in heaven,
Where lovers never part.

Down in that lonesome valley,
Where the flowers fade an' bloom,
There lies my own sweet Pearly
In the cold an' silent tomb.

Murder by Knife / 6

Robert Wood, a young commercial artist, was accused of the murder of Phyllis Dimmock, a prostitute, at her flat in St. Paul's Road (subsequently renamed Agar Grove), Camden Town, London, in the early hours of Thursday, 12 September 1907. Partly due to Wood's personable appearance, but also to the efforts of his counsel, Marshall Hall, and the less-than-scrupulous solicitor, Arthur Newton, he was the first man to give evidence on his own behalf in a capital case (under the Criminal Evidence Act 1898) and be acquitted. The popularity of the verdict, and of Wood himself, is reflected in this verse:

A sketch of Mr. Justice Grantham made by Robert Wood during the summing-up at his trial

So you think that Bob's a killer?
Don't be silly—he just *couldn't*.
You can say all night, 'twas Robert Wood,
And I'll say Robert Woodn't.

And the general "she's-a-Judas" attitude towards Wood's girlfriend, who had been forced to inform the police of his connection with Phyllis Dimmock, is expressed in perhaps the briefest crhyme of all, which was chanted by the crowd outside the court when the verdict became known:

Ruby Young
Should be hung.

Three hours later, at eleven o'clock, sections of the crowd were still chanting that and singing "Ruby, Ruby, won't you come out tonight?" (to the tune of "Daisy") as she was smuggled out in the dress of an Old Bailey charwoman.

Murder by Mallet

Letter published in the *Daily Mirror*, 9 June 1967:

> Every now and again I play an old gramophone record
> bought back in the Thirties. On one side is a song called
> "Dark Haired Marie" and on the reverse side is "You
> Brought My Heart the Sunshine."
>
> The singer is the late Frank Titterton and his accom-
> panist and the writer of the lyrics is named as
> "Lozanne."
>
> They are such melancholy songs that I wondered if
> you . . . could give any clue as to the composer's life.
>
> BALLAD-MONGER

"Lozanne" was the pen name of Mrs. Alma Victoria Rat-
tenbury, an attractive Canadian woman whose talents as a pi-
anist far outweighed her gifts as a lyric writer. She and her
husband, Francis, a semiretired architect, came to England in
1928, and settled down in a small house called Villa Madeira,
in Manor Road, Bournemouth. She was then thirty-one years
of age, her husband about sixty.

In September 1934, the Rattenburys advertised in a local
paper for a "daily willing lad, 14–18, for housework; scout-
trained preferred," and George Percy Stoner, who became
eighteen in November, was engaged as a chauffeur-handyman.
Within weeks, he and Mrs. Rattenbury were lovers.

On the night of Sunday, 24 March 1935, Francis Ratten-
bury was savagely beaten about the head as he sat sleeping in
an armchair in the drawing room. While under the influence
of alcohol and morphia (the latter administered by a doctor),
Mrs. Rattenbury made several statements to the effect that

she was solely responsible for the crime. Charged with doing grievous bodily harm with intent to murder, she was removed to Holloway Prison. Four days later, Stoner also was arrested, but this time the charge was murder, for Francis Rattenbury had died earlier in the day.

Awaiting trial, Mrs. Rattenbury composed a song called "By Some Mistake." She told a friend: "I kept repeating the extraordinary words over and over again to help keep my mind sane."

> By some mistake my spirit held you, dear,
> But now I wake to agony and fear,
> To fading hope and thought distressed and grey;
> With outstretched hand I put your face away.
>
> By some mistake you filled my empty days,
> But now I wake to face the parting ways.
> I see your smile, I hear the words you say;
> With no reply, I hush your voice away.
>
> By some mistake, by some divine mistake,
> I dreamed awhile, but now I wake, I wake.
> Yet, dying, dream you kept my vision true;
> I seem to climb to heav'n in loving you.

At the trial (before Mr. Justice Humphreys at the Old Bailey, 27 May 1935), Mrs. Rattenbury and Stoner refused to inculpate each other. The prosecution sought to prove that the crime was the result of a plot, but it soon became clear that Stoner, motivated by jealousy, had attacked Francis Rattenbury with a mallet that he had borrowed quite openly from his grandmother, and that Mrs. Rattenbury had had no foreknowledge of the crime and had taken no part in it. After a retirement of forty-seven minutes, the jury acquitted Mrs. Rattenbury, and brought in a verdict of guilty against Stoner, with a recommendation to mercy.[1]

Four days later, Mrs. Rattenbury travelled to Christchurch, Hampshire; there, having waded into a quiet tributary of the Avon, she committed suicide by plunging a knife six times into her chest. The following extracts are from letters that were found in her handbag:

If I only thought it would help Stoner I would stay on, but it has been pointed out to me all too vividly I cannot help him. That is my death sentence. . . . Eight o'clock. After so much walking I have got here. Oh to see the swans and spring flowers and just smell them. And how singular I should have chosen the spot Stoner said he nearly jumped out of the train once at. It was not intentional my coming here. I tossed a coin, like Stoner always did, and it came down Christchurch. It is beautiful here. What a lovely world we are in! It must be easier to be hanged than to have to do the job oneself. . . . One must be bold to do a thing like this. It is beautiful here and I am alone. Thank God for peace at last.

Stoner was reprieved. A model prisoner, he was released in 1942, when he was still only twenty-six. He continues to live in the Bournemouth area.

NOTE

1. See *Trial of Rattenbury and Stoner* (Hodge, 1935)—particularly the brilliant Introduction by F. Tennyson Jesse.

Murder by Poison / 1

"Impudent" seems an inappropriate word to describe a mur-
derer—a multicide at that—but it certainly applies to Dr.
William Palmer, executed on 14 June 1856 for the murder of
John Parsons Cook, owner of a mare called Polestar that had
won a race at Shrewsbury, providing him with funds that
were desperately needed by Palmer to pay off creditors and a
woman blackmailer. The first postmortem examination of
Cook's body—at which Palmer, astonishingly enough, was al-
lowed to be present—is like the product of a collaboration be-
tween Mary Shelley and Ben Travers. At the trial, Dr. John
Thomas Harland testified:

> When the intestines and stomach were being placed in
> the jar, and while Mr. Devonshire was opening the stom-
> ach, I noticed Palmer pushed Mr. Newton on to Mr. De-
> vonshire, and he shook a portion of the contents of the
> stomach into the body. I thought a joke was passing
> among them, and I said, "Do not do that," to the whole.
> Palmer was the only one close to them when Mr. Newton
> and Mr. Devonshire were pushed together. After this in-
> terruption the opening of the stomach proceeded. It
> contained about, I should think, 2 or 3 ounces of brown-
> ish liquid. It was stated that there was nothing particu-
> lar found in the stomach, and Palmer remarked to Mr.
> Bamford, "They will not hang us yet." The stomach was
> then emptied into a jar along with the stomach itself.
> The intestines . . . were placed in the jar, with their con-
> tents, as they were taken from the body. I then tied the
> jar over with two bladders and sealed it, and placed it on
> the table beside the body. At that time Palmer was mov-
> ing about the room. My attention had been called away

"The Accurst Surgeon"

by the examination, and I missed the jar for a few min-
utes. I called out, "Where is the jar?" and Palmer, from
the other end of the room, said, "It is here." Palmer was
standing a yard or two from a door at the end of the
room. I got the jar from him. I found there was a cut,
hardly an inch long, through both bladders. The cut was
quite clean, as if nothing had passed through. I asked
who had done this, and Palmer, Mr. Devonshire, and Mr.
Newton all seemed to say they had not done it.

Two days later, Palmer offered a postboy £10 to upset the
jar when he was taking it to the railway station; the bribe was
not accepted. Also he persuaded the local postmaster to open
and read the letter containing the analysis, and then wrote to
the coroner, quoting a passage from the analysis which said
that no strychnine was found in the body, and suggesting that
a verdict of natural death would save a lot of bother. During
the inquest, he sent the coroner several presents of game.

The following ballad was widely circulated during the fort-
night between the end of the trial and the execution.

The Life and Trial of Palmer

Oh, listen unto William Palmer
Who does in anguish sore bewail,
Now guilty they at last have found me,
And sent me back to Stafford Jail.[1]
Everyone appears against me,
Every person does me hate,
What excitement is impending
On guilty William Palmer's fate.

Chorus

My trial causes great excitement
In town and country everywhere.
Now guilty found is William Palmer
Of Rugeley town in Staffordshire.

Many years I was a sportsman,
Many wondrous deeds I've done,
Many a race I have attended,
Many a thousand lost and won.[2]
They say I poisoned my wife's mother,
And took away her precious life,
And slew poor Cook and my own brother,
And poisoned my own lawful wife.[3]

Everything looks black against me,
That I really must confess.
The very thoughts that do oppress me

Cause me agony and distress.
Now the jury did convict me
And prove I did commit the deed,
And, sentence passed on William Palmer,
To Stafford I was sent with speed.

In Rugeley I was once respected,
A gentleman, lived at my ease,
With noblemen I was connected,
And sporting men of all degrees.
Although a doctor, no one knew me
To do anything amiss.
Now each one strives to undo me,
I never thought I'd come to this.

My poor old mother now at Rugeley,
My awful end must now bewail,
To know her son must die with scorn,
A felon's death in Stafford Jail.
Every charge alleged against me
I have strongly it denied,
Twelve long days my trial lasted,
And now I am condemned to die.

Dreadful is my situation,
Before the awful bar I stand,
I might have filled a noble station,
Unfortunate, unhappy man.
Infants yet unborn will mention,
When to manhood they appear,
The name of Dr. William Palmer
Of Rugeley town in Staffordshire.

Will no one sympathize with Palmer,
Who every charge did strong deny,
You are all aware I am found guilty,
For by a jury I've been tried.
My situation makes me tremble,
I am borne down with grief and care,
All conversation is of Palmer
Of Rugeley town in Staffordshire.[4]

1. From the Old Bailey. The feeling against him in Staffordshire was so strong than an act was passed (19 Vic cap 16, afterwards known as "Palmer's Act") which allowed a trial to be transferred to a different venue.

2. The way in which Sir Alexander Cockburn presented the case for the Crown, leaving no doubt as to the verdict, was described by Palmer in race-course parlance: "It was the riding that did it." And he told the governor of Stafford Prison: "When the jury returned into court, and I saw the cocked-up nose of the perky little foreman, I knew it was a gooser with me."

3. To name but a few. He is thought to have killed many others, including an uncle, who died after a "brandy drinking match," some creditors, and several of his legitimate and illegitimate children.

4. The people of Rugeley, horrified at the notoriety that Palmer had brought on the town, sent a deputation to the prime minister, asking permission to change its name. "Certainly," Palmerston replied. "Why not name it after me?" The idea was dropped.

Murder by Poison / 2

From the *Stockport Advertiser,* 11 December 1863:

Alice Hewitt, alias Holt, was indicted for the wilful murder of Mary Bailey, her mother, at Stockport, on the 27th March last. . . . The prisoner was a widow, and for some time before her mother's death had been cohabiting with a man named Holt, passing as his wife. The deceased was also a widow, and resided with Holt and her daughter at 43 Great Egerton Street, Heaton Norris, in the borough of Stockport. The prisoner was in poor circumstances, and she and Holt evidently regarded her mother as an encumbrance.

There appears to be considerable competition between the life insurance offices at Stockport. Of these there is one called the Wesleyan and General Assurance Society, which insures for very small sums, and receives the premiums in weekly and fortnightly payments; sixpence a week, it seems, would insure £28 on death. The prisoner had been canvassed for this society in January last, and on the 18th February, her mother falling unwell from bronchitis, she agreed to insure. The mother did not recover sufficiently to go before the doctor, so the prisoner applied to a lodger, Ann Bailey, to go with her and pass the doctor as her mother. Ann Bailey refused, and she then said she would send for Betty Wood, as Garlick, the canvasser for the society, had told her anyone would do to pass the doctor. She did not send for Wood, but got one Elizabeth Wells to go with her to Peter Scarlett's, the agent of the society, and represented Wells to be her mother. The examination was passed, and the necessary certificate was obtained from the medical man.

The deceased was attended by the union surgeon, and up to the 1st March was improving. The insurance was effected on the 6th March. On the 12th the Infirmary surgeon visited the deceased and found her suffering from sickness. She said she had great pain in her stomach. Ann Bailey was about this time sent on several occasions for some pies, which were always warmed by the prisoner, and it was observed that they caused vomiting in all who partook of them. The Infirmary surgeon varied his remedies, but without arresting the symptoms, and he observed that the medicine was not regularly given to the deceased. The union surgeon was also attending the deceased, but neither of the surgeons knew that the other was visiting her.

The woman died on the 27th March, early in the morning. The symptoms were consistent with arsenical poisoning, and not with bronchitis. A few days before the old woman died, one Catherine Ryan was in the house, and saw the prisoner throw some of the medicine into the fire. Ryan said, "I'd never go for medicine and throw it away." The prisoner said, "H——to them and their medicine." She went up to bed, and in coming down again said, "Is my mother dead?" Ryan said, "No, nor signs of it. It is to be hoped she'll recover." The prisoner said, "Tut, tut, Mrs. Ryan."

The daughter also, it seems, bought some arsenic at the shop of Mr. Davenport, a druggist. On one occasion, having bought some arsenic, she said to Ann Bailey, "Ann, you mustn't say anything at all about this here." Bailey said, "About what?" She said, "About this arsenic," and Bailey said, "No." That evening, about nine o'clock, the prisoner asked her mother if she would have some brandy and water, and she said, "yes." The prisoner then went out with a cup, and after an absence of half an hour returned with some brandy in the cup, but would not let her mother drink of it for some time, as she said she had grated a root into it and wanted it to dissolve. When the mother took the brandy, the prisoner seemed vexed that she had not drunk up the dregs, and this cup was afterwards found strongly impregnated with arsenic.

When the old woman died the prisoner went into Ann Bailey's room, and said, "Well, Ann, I am very glad my mother's dead. I've all my clothes fast (pawned), and I wanted this money to release them. If she had not died it would have been God help us." She also said, "If she had not got the money, her husband (Holt) would have beaten her."

On the 8th April Scarlett paid the prisoner £25, the amount of the insurance money. The deceased was disinterred on the 12th June, in consequence of the discovery of the fraud that had been practiced on the insurance company and of various rumors that were in circulation, and it was found fully impregnated with arsenic. 130 grains were found in the body, twenty-six times as much as would destroy life. . . .

The jury, after an absence of twenty minutes, found the prisoner GUILTY, with a recommendation to mercy. On hearing the verdict the prisoner fainted, and moaned in a way pitiful to hear.

His Lordship assumed the black cap, and, after a few appropriate remarks suitable to so solemn an occasion, and promising to forward the recommendation of the jury to the proper quarter, although he could hold out no hope that the prayer would be complied with, he proceeded to sentence the prisoner to DEATH.

The wretched woman was then removed from the dock in an insensible condition.

While the court was dispersing, the "public" manifested considerable feeling against the witness Holt. They cried, "Fetch him out," and looked as though they were prepared to offer violence to him on his appearance outside; but, by the advice of some person connected with the prosecution, who noticed this hostile expression, he jumped into the dock and made his way through the gaol. Thence, by changing his hat to disguise himself, he managed to escape to the railway station.

The execution of Alice Holt, which took place a few days later, inspired a ballad that is still sung at the Player's (music-hall) Theatre, London.

A dreadful case of murder,
Such as we seldom hear,
Committed was at Stockport,
In the Country of Cheshire;
Where a mother named Mary Bailey
They did so cruelly slaughter,
By poison administered all in her beer
By her own daughter.

The daughter insured the life of the mother
For twenty-six pounds at her death,
Then she and the man that she lived with
Determined to take away her breath.
And when Betty Wood represented the mother[1]
She didn't act with propriety,
For the poor mother lost her life,
And they all swindled the Society.

Now that the old gal's life's insured,
Holt to the daughter did say,
Better in the grave she were immured,
And the money will make us gay.
Now that you have got me in the family way,
And from me my virtue you've wrung,
You'll never be happy a day
Till on the gallows I'm hung.

She laid a plan to murder her,
As we now see so clear,
To put a quantity of arsenic
Into her poor mother's beer.
To see her lay in agony
Upon that dreadful night,
With a dreadful dose of arsenic,
Oh, it was a dreadful sight.

She lived but just six hours,
Then the poor woman did die,
And this base murdering wretch
The dreadful deed did deny.
On the man Holt she laid the blame,

Vowed he did her mother slay,
Holt on her did the same,
Saying she took the mother's life away.

But there's no doubt the base wretch
Did her poor mother slay,
For which on Chester's scaffold
Her life did forfeit pay:
So all young women a warning take
By this poor wretch you see,
A hanging for the mother's sake
On Chester's fatal tree.

NOTE

1. William J. Skillern, former Head of Reference Services, Stockport, suggests that "if Elizabeth Well's name be written as 'Betty Wells', it is not very different from 'Betty Wood', and it is possible that the writer of the verses was confused over the two names."

Murder by Poison / 3

Charles Bravo, a thirty-year-old barrister, collapsed at his home, The Priory, Balham, shortly after drinking four glasses of burgundy with a dinner of whiting, roast lamb, and anchovy eggs on toast.[1] He died, after three days of agony, on Friday, 21 April 1876. At an inquest held privately at the Priory, the jury returned a verdict that "the deceased had died of antimonial poisoning, but there was no evidence to show how it got into his body." Many people, however—chief among them, Bravo's father—were dissatisfied with the attempted secrecy of the inquest. And with the verdict. They felt that there was evidence that Bravo had been murdered, and that three people were involved. First and foremost of these was Florence Bravo, to whom Charles had been married for five months; a wealthy woman (she had inherited £40,000 from her first husband, Captain Alexander Ricardo, a Grenadier Guardsman, who had died of alcoholism in 1871), she had, after Ricardo's death, been the mistress of sixty-four-year-old Dr. James Manby Gully, who now lived close by. Florence's maid, Mrs. Jane Cannon Cox, a forty-three-year-old Anglo-Indian widow, was the third of the suspicious trio. A parody of Goldsmith's "On Woman" adumbrated a possible motive and method:

> When lovely woman stoops to folly
> And finds her husband in the way,
> What charm can soothe her melancholy,
> What art can turn him into clay?
>
> The only means her aims to cover
> And save herself from prison locks,

And repossess her ancient lover,
Are Burgundy and Mrs. Cox.

Prompted by the public disquiet, the lord chief justice quashed the findings of the first inquest and ordered another inquiry, at which, after an absence of three and three-quarter hours, the jury returned the verdict: "We find that Charles Delauney Turner Bravo did not commit suicide; that he was wilfully murdered by the administering of tartar emetic, but there is not sufficient evidence to fix the guilt upon any person or persons." In other words, Florence and Mrs. Cox were guilty, but there was no way of proving it.

NOTE

1. An investigation into the eating habits of murderees might provide interesting data for the new victimologists. Poison apart, is there some connection between what they eat and the way they die? Certainly, a glance through some of the last menus shows that many of the victims had appetites which, to say the least of them, were unconventional. (See the Borden breakfast, pages 5–6). The best trencherman of all, and by a long chalk, was Edwin Bartlett, who died on New Year's Eve, 1885, from drinking liquid chloroform. Writing of his last few meals in her book *Blood in the Parlor* (Thomas Yoseloff, 1964), Dorothy Dunbar comments:

> The thought of necrosis did not seem to affect his appetite. Mr. Bartlett had oysters for lunch, a jugged hare for dinner, and for those who are interested in the "virility-through-oysters" theory his supper consisted of more oysters, bread and butter, mango chutney, and cake. . . . He said he was feeling better and ordered a large haddock for breakfast the next morning, telling the maid, Alice Fulcher, he should get up an hour earlier at the thought of having it.

Raymond Chandler, discussing the difficulty of getting the average person to swallow and retain liquid chloroform, wrote:

> Edwin is a little bit different from us. You can feed anything to Edwin, and all he wants is to get up an hour early the next morning and start eating more. I think the man had a stomach like a goat. I think he could digest sawdust, old tin cans, iron filings and shoe leather. I think he could drink chloroform just like you and I could drink orange juice. (*Raymond Chandler Speaking*, Hamish Hamilton, 1962).

The Bartlett case does not figure in this collection, but, as a footnote to this footnote, it is worth quoting one of the verses written by the Rev. George Dyson, "der udder" member of that strange *ménage à trois* in Pimlico, to Adelaide Bartlett, Edwin's wife:

Who is it that hath burst the door,
Unclosed the heart that shut before,
And set her queen-like on its throne,
And made its homage all her own?—
                                    My Birdie.

Murder by Poison / 4

In August 1889, at Liverpool Assizes, American-born Mrs. Florence Maybrick was found guilty of murdering her husband with arsenic. The evidence against her, more suppositional than circumstantial, was weak—indeed, it was never really established that James Maybrick, a Liverpool cotton broker who had for years been dosing his hypochondria with strychnine and arsenic, had not died a natural death—and one can only assume that the jury was influenced by a blunder-filled and blurred summing-up by Mr. Justice Stephen, and that evidence concerning an affair Mrs. Maybrick had been having with a man named Brierley, with whom she had spent three nights in a London hotel and to whom she had written an ambiguously worded letter about her husband's illness, clouded their minds with moral issues.

The verdict caused a furor on both sides of the Atlantic. There were protest meetings, petitions for reprieve, letters to *The Times* from doctors and lawyers—and verses, of course. One of the verses, by a woman, ran:

> Men of the Saxon race,
> Armed by this foul disgrace,
> Pure yourself, heart and face!
> Hurl the first stone.
>
> Heed not a woman's cry,
> Heed not humanity;
> Stand! Watch a weak one die!
> Hurl the last stone.
>
> Up, men of truth! and save
> Her from a culprit's grave;

Over her kindly wave
Justice, charity.

An enterprising Liverpool printer produced a double-sided broadsheet that catered for both factions; it was up to the customer to choose sides. Either for Mrs. Maybrick:

> We only ask for justice,
> No fear or favor shown,
> But that is not conspicuous
> In the Maybrick case, you'll own.
>
> The law says quite distinctly
> That if there a doubt should be,
> Then give it to the prisoner
> And let that prisoner free.

Or against her:

> The greatest trial of modern times
> At last is at an end,
> And in spite of Sir Charles's[1]
> Mighty efforts to defend,
>
> The jury in their verdict
> Very quietly did agree,
> And soon with Mrs. Maybrick
> It will be U.P.[2]

Little more than a week before the date set for the execution, Florence Maybrick was reprieved. Edgar Lustgarten comments:[3]

At that time reprieves were not come by two a penny, nor was there much squeamishness at the thought of hanging women. Mrs. Maybrick's neck was saved for the most logical of reasons: because the case against her fell short of legal proof. "Although," said the Home Secretary, "the evidence leads clearly to the conclusion that the prisoner administered, and attempted to administer, arsenic to her husband with intent to murder, yet it does not wholly exclude a reasonable doubt whether his death was in fact caused by the administration of arsenic."

If there was "reasonable doubt," she was not guilty of murder. That was the only indictment upon which she had been tried. The life sentence was administratively imposed for an attempt to murder with which she had not been charged.

Until the reprieve, the verses had been almost wholeheartedly in her favor, but with the announcement of the home secretary's decision, several appeared which suggested that, considering the looseness of her morals, Mrs. Maybrick had gotten off lightly:

Penal Servitude for Mrs. Maybrick
She will not have to climb Golden Stairs

The Maybrick trial is over now, there's been a lot of jaw,
Of doctors' contradiction, and expounding of the law;
She had Sir Charles Russell to defend her, as we know,
But though he tried his very best, it all turned out no go.

Chorus

But Mrs. Maybrick will not have to climb the golden stairs;
The jury found her guilty so she nearly said her prayers;
She's at another kind of mashing and at it she must stop.
Old Berry[4] is took down a peg with his big long drop.

Now, the doctors at the trial had a very gay old time,
They all told different stories about this cruel crime.
Some said that Mr. Maybrick to death had dosed himself,
While others said it was his wife that put him on the shelf.

Then came the servant's story of how the flypapers were
found,
In fact, it seems the missus had arsenic all round,
In food and drink of every kind, in cupboard and in box,
In handkerchiefs and even in the pockets of her frocks.

Next came the waiter's story about her trip to town,
Which proved that from the virtue of a woman she had fell
down,

And when a woman like her from her husband goes astray,
It plainly shows she wishes that he was out of the way.

Then came the fatal letter that fairly cooked her goose,
It seemed to say to Brierley that she would soon be loose;
And though she made a statement to explain it all away,
The jury wouldn't have it, she the penalty must pay.

Then to each gay and flirty wife may this a warning be:
Don't write to any other man or sit upon his knee;
When once you start like Mrs. Maybrick perhaps you couldn't
    stop,
So stick close to your husband and keep clear of Berry's drop.

The years went by, and despite efforts to obtain her release,
Mrs. Maybrick remained in prison. There was a widely held
belief that Queen Victoria, who had expressed disapproval of
Mrs. Maybrick, was responsible for the long sentence. When
the queen died, the following verses by Ophelia Lawrence
Blair were published in the *Louisville Evening Post:*

God's Justice Will Be Done

The faces of the multitude waxed dim;
Their sorrows died into a distant strain.
No fair face shone in love, no soothing hymn;
No fond voice satisfied her lonely pain.

A nation's gifts were spread above a grave,
A nation's honor's heaped upon a crown.
In Woking Prison no hand came to save
The Prisoner, Florence Maybrick, from the queenly frown.

Not for her was womanly compassion shown,
Far from America she sits today alone.

Florence Maybrick was released from prison in 1904, and
she returned to the United States. For some twenty-five years
before her death in 1941, she lived alone in a shack at South
Kent, Connecticut, with an assortment of cats to keep her
company.

1. Sir Charles Russell.
2. Quoted in *Etched in Arsenic*, Trevor Christie, Harrap, 1969.
3. *Verdict in Dispute*, Wingate, 1949.
4. James Berry, the hangman; see page 224.

Murder by Poison / 5

If Dr. Hawley Harley Crippen had kept his nerve, he might well have gotten away with the killing of his wife Cora.[1] The police, headed by the not over-efficient Chief Inspector Walter Dew, had questioned him about his wife's disappearance and had searched his house at 39 Hilldrop Crescent,[2] Camden Town, when Crippen himself disappeared, taking with him his twenty-seven-year-old mistress, Ethel Le Neve. A further search of the house revealed portions of Mrs. Crippen's body in the cellar, and a postmortem examination showed that death was due to a massive overdose of the narcotic poison, hyoscine. A warrant was issued for the arrest of Crippen and Le Neve ("Wanted for Murder and Mutilation"). A week after the discovery of the crime, the captain of the Quebec-bound SS *Montrose*, suspecting that two passengers travelling as "Mr. Robinson and son" were the wanted couple, sent a radio message to London (the first time that radio telegraphy was used in a murder hunt). The news of this prompted the following lines, which were sung to the tune of a popular song of the period (1910), "Has Anybody Here Seen Kelly?":

> Has anybody here seen Crippen,
> C R I double-P E N?
> Has anybody here seen Crippen?—
> Seek him up and down.
> He's done a bunk to Canada
> And left his wife in a coal cellar.
> Has anybody here seen Crippen,
> Crippen from Camden Town?

Chief Inspector Dew travelled on a faster ship to Quebec and boarded the *Montrose* at Father Point. He had no difficulty in recognizing the clean-shaven "Mr. Robinson" as the

THE WESTERN UNION TELEGRAPH COMPANY.
THE LARGEST TELEGRAPHIC SYSTEM IN EXISTENCE.

DIRECT ROUTE FOR ALL PARTS OF THE UNITED STATES.
CANADA, CENTRAL AMERICA, WEST INDIES,
SOUTH AMERICA, & VIA THE PACIFIC CABLE TO AUSTRALIA,
NEW ZEALAND, FANNING, FIJI AND NORFOLK ISLANDS.

ATLANTIC CABLES direct to CANADA and to NEW YORK CITY.
DIRECT WIRES TO ALL THE PRINCIPAL CITIES.

No.	Service Instructions.	Time Received.	
1928	Col	8 46/	WESTERN UNION TELEGRAPH Co. 31 JUL 1910 EFFINGHAM HOUSE, ARUNDEL ST, STRAND, W.C.

Handed in at

Montrose via Father Point Que 10

CABLE OFFICE: EFFINGHAM HOUSE, ARUNDEL ST,
STRAND.

To   Handcuffs Ldn Eng

Crippen and leneve
arrested wire later
Dew

To
Mrs R.D. Lowns & Son,
12 Ashbrook Grove, Upper Holloway

I authorize my Solicitor Mr Arthur
Newton to sell the whole of my
furniture & effects at 39 Hilldrop
Crescent, & to pay the 2 quarters
rent, which will become due on
the 29th of September, & also the Gas Bill
& Water Rate —

1. September 1910.

H.H. Crippen

A note written from prison

previously mustached Crippen, and "Master Robinson" as
Ethel Le Neve wearing male clothes (the trousers adjusted to
her size by safety pins). They were arrested and, following ex-
tradition proceedings, brought back to England.

This oddly shaped verse was inspired, it seems, by a
Press picture showing Dew and Crippen together on the Liver-
pool quayside and Ethel Le Neve being escorted down the
gangplank:

Miss Le Neve, old Dew is waiting
On the wall for you at Liverpool,
And he says he saw you sitting
On the knee of Dr. Crippen,
Dressed in boy's clothes,
On the Montrose,
Miss Le Neve.

After a three-day trial at the Old Bailey, Crippen was convicted of his wife's murder. Ethel Le Neve, tried separately as an accessory, was acquitted. In the condemned cell at Pentonville Prison, Crippen wrote love letters to Ethel, calling her "wifie" (her pet name for him was "hub"). He also wrote poems, only one of which seems to have survived:

When the heart is breaking, and the way is long,
In seeking rest, with no accompanying song,
Scorn of the world, by cruel Fate undone,
Friendless, yet not alone—for there is one—

Who truly loves this soon admitted clay,
Who truly dreads the sure and awful day
When mortal soul shall fly to realms aloft.
In life—in death—she still shall speak me soft.

On 23 November 1910, the day of Crippen's execution, Ethel emigrated to Canada, calling herself Miss Allen. She returned to England during the Great War under the name Ethel Nelson and soon afterwards married a man named Stanley Smith, a clerk in the furniture shop where she herself worked as a typist. The Smiths had two children. (A few years ago, I traced them—in furtherance of a book called *The Crippen File*, Allison & Busby, 1985. Until then, they were unaware of their mother's part in the Crippen case: she had never breathed a word of it.) In 1967, Mrs. Smith, a widow, died in Dulwich Hospital; her last request, so the story goes, was that a locket holding a picture of Crippen should be buried with her.

In May 1961, a "music-hall musical" entitled *Belle,* which was based on the Crippen case, opened at the Strand Theatre, London. Music and lyrics were by Monty Norman, and the book was adapted by Wolf Mankowitz from a play by Beverley Cross. Crippen, described in the introductory notes as "one of the great lovers of forensic history," was played by George Benson. Acting as a form of chorus, a character named Lasher, a music-hall comedian and one of Belle's beaux, sang "The Ballad of Doctor Crippen" as a link between scenes. The following are extracts:

> Here's a little story,
> A touching tale of woe:
> Happened here in London
> 'Bout fifty years ago.
> A little Yankee doctor
> Created quite a din,
> All because he gave his
> Dear wife a Mickie-Finn.
> Funny little dentist,
> Crippen was his name,
> Pulled his patients' teeth out
> With very little pain.
> In his little surgery
> He was so up-to-date—
> Ultra-modern equipment
> To do you while you wait.
> Ethel was his sweetheart,
> His secretary and nurse;
> He loved her by appointment
> But flies got in the ointment
> When that handsome Lasher
> Had had enough of Belle.
>
> Funny little fellow,
> Crippen was his name.
> Might not get to Canada—
> Let's hope so just the same.

Poor old Doctor Crippen,
The net is closing in;
Someone on the Montrose
Has set the police on him.

Funny little fellow,
Ethel by his side,
There in the Old Bailey
For murder they were tried.

When the trial was over,
The jury, sad to tell,
Found old Crippen guilty
Of killing poor old Belle.

Then one early morning
The hangman took his toll;
May the Lord have mercy
On poor old Crippen's soul.

Funny little Fellow,
Crippen was his name;
See him for a sixpence
In the Hall of Fame.

NOTES

1. Better known by her stage name of Belle Elmore (although she made few professional appearances as a soprano, most of them during an "artistes" strike).

2. This address, probably the most famous in the annals of crime, no longer exists. The house, damaged by a bomb during World War II, was demolished in 1953, and there is not even a blue plaque to mark the site. The small block of council flats that was erected there—which surely should have been called Crippen Court, Le Neve's Folly, or Belle End—is known as Margaret Bondfield House. Islington Borough Council, it seems, has no sense of history.

Murder by Poison / 6

Early in 1916, at the swank apartment in Manhattan that he had received as part of a dowry fewer than eighteen months before, Arthur Warren Waite, a personable young dentist who pretended that he was a doctor, an eminent one at that, used poison, probably arsenic, to murder his mother-in-law, and then, within six weeks, used arsenic, no doubt about it, to murder his millionaire father-in-law. It seems likely that, but for the fact that he was not his usual, excessively charming self when distant in-laws came to the apartment to offer condolences (thereby causing one of them to question—*à la* Wilde's Lady Bracknell—the naturalness of the rather sudden orphaning of his wife), he would have contrived to make himself a wealthy widower, able unfurtively to enjoy further hours of boudoir bliss with a scarlet matron of his long and comprehensive acquaintance. The offended in-law's questioning led to a police investigation—and that to the trial of Waite for double murder—and that to his removal to the Sing Sing penitentiary, where, on Thursday, 24 May 1917 (following a number of postponements that, by American appellate standards, added up to alacrity), he was executed. Shortly before that shocking end, he, understandably still a solipsist, wrote a poem that he dedicated to himself—"an address to his body by his soul after death":

> And thou art dead, dear comrade,
> In whom I dwelt a time;
> With whom I strolled through star-kissed bowers
> Of fragrant jessamine.
> And thou wert weak, O comrade—
> Thyself in self did fail—

And now the stars are turned to tears,
And sobs the nightingale.
And though I now must leave you,
The same old songs I'll sing,
And o'er yon hill the same soft dew
Will spread its silver wing.
Across the fields, among the stars,
I now must go alone;
Your spirit now will roam afar,
And leave you, friend, alone.[1]

NOTE

1. Quoted by Richard Whittington-Egan in his sufficient essay on the case, "Dentist in the Chair," which appears in my anthology, *The Medical Murders* (Piatkus, 1991).

Murder by Poison / 7

In December 1966, at Freehold, a dismal little town in New Jersey, Carl Coppolino, a doctor and anesthetist who had written authoritatively on the medical uses of hypnosis, was tried for the murder of his mistress's husband, Colonel William Farber. The case for the prosecution depended largely upon the evidence of Mrs. Marjorie Farber, who, having been jilted by Coppolino after his wife's death, testified that she had assisted him in murdering her husband, she being under hypnosis from Coppolino at the time.

The prosecution sought to prove that the colonel had been poisoned with a rare and grotesquely named chemical, succinyldicholine chloride, a quantity of which Coppolino had obtained "for experiments on dogs"; and for two days Dr. Milton Helpern, Chief Medical Examiner to the City of New York, and his chief toxicologist gave evidence—in effect, an illustrated lecture—on the postmortem results of the poison. An American friend, the late Robert F. Hussey (author of a good book on the Wallace murder case, *Murderer Scot-Free*, David & Charles, 1972), wrote to me soon after the trial of Coppolino:

> The reporters were less than discreet in their "taste" after seeing Helpern juggling the colonel's disinterred larynx for a couple of days, the pauses in post-mortem testimony being taken up with endless exhibitions on a screen of micro-photographs of the colonel's sliced-by-microtome arteries, all in color, of course. Drinks and macabre songs were clearly the only evening antidote for the Press.

One of the songs, composed by an unknown reporter and sung to the tune of "Smile the While," went like this:

Smile the while you slice my heart in two;
When the trial rolls by I'll say adieu.
Put me back into my grave
With all the parts you'd like to save.
This has been a funny time for me,
Waxed and sliced for everyone to see.
Farewell, Carl and Marjorie-e-e,
'Til we meet again-n-n.

Coppolino was acquitted of the murder of Colonel Farber; but in the following year, this time in Florida, he was convicted of murdering his wife with the same kind of poison. After this second trial, with Coppolino serving a life sentence, the district attorney of Monmouth County, New Jersey, asked the grand jury to indict Mrs. Farber for the murder of her husband, but they voted a "no bill" on the grounds of insufficient evidence.

Coppolino was released from prison in 1979, and in the following year published his version of the events, *The Crime That Never Was* (Justice Press, Florida).

Murder by Rock

The Arran Murder—the killing of Edwin Rose by John Watson Laurie, a fellow vacationer, on Monday, 15 July 1889—was one of William Roughead's favorite cases.[1] After Laurie's arrest, this parody of a well-known hymn was widely circulated in and around Glasgow:

> I do believe and shall believe
> That Laurie killed poor Rose,
> And on Goat Fell he shed his blood
> And stole away his clothes.

Laurie was found guilty and sentenced to death, but was reprieved on the grounds of insanity; he died in Perth Prison in 1930, when he was sixty-nine. An interesting Arran superstition was mentioned at the trial: the local police had buried Rose's boots in the sand in the belief that this would prevent his ghost from walking.

NOTE

1. See *Trial of J. W. Laurie* (Hodge, 1932), which Roughead edited; also his essay, "The Arran Murder," which appears in, among other books, my own anthology, *The Pleasures of Murder* (Sphere, 1986).

Murder by Rope (Lynching)

This song, "Strange Fruit," was featured in *Hang Down Your Head and Die* (see page 233):

> Southern trees bear a strange fruit:
> Blood on the leaves and blood at the root,
> Black bodies swinging in the Southern Breeze;
> Strange fruit hanging from the poplar trees.
>
> Pastoral scene of the gallant South,
> The bulging eyes and the twisted mouth;
> Scent of magnolias sweet and fresh:
> Then the sudden smell of burning flesh.
>
> Here is a fruit for the crows to pluck,
> For the rain to gather, for the wind to suck,
> For the sun to rot, for a tree to drop:
> Here is a strange and bitter crop.

LEWIS ALLEN

Murder by Rope
(Legal Murder)

"The Campden Wonder" is the traditional name for the strange goings-on at Chipping Campden, Gloucestershire, from August 1660. William Harrison, steward to the lady of the manor, set out to collect rents from outlying tenants and did not return; circumstantial evidence indicated that he had been robbed and murdered. John Perry, servant to the Harrisons, was suspected, and, when examined by a justice of the peace, confessed to being an accessory to Harrison's murder, accusing his mother and brother as the principals. All three were tried and hanged. Two years later, William Harrison reappeared with a picturesque but scarcely credible explanation for his disappearance.

The case has fascinated many writers,[1] including John Masefield, who, in his plays *The Campden Wonder* and *Mrs. Harrison*, suggested possible explanations for the double mystery.

In 1945, E. O. Winstedt announced the discovery of new evidence in the Bodleian Library;[2] this evidence included a broadsheet ballad probably published in 1662:

Truth brought to Light: OR,
Wonderful strange and true news from Gloucester shire, concerning one Mr. William Harrison, formerly Stewart to the Lady Nowell of Cambden, who was supposed to be Murthered by the Widow Pery and two of her Sons, one of which was Servant to the said Gentleman. Therefore they were all three apprehended and sent to Gloucester Gaol, and about two years since arraigned, found guilty, condemned, and Executed upon Broadway hill in sight of Cambden, the mother and one

Son being then buried under the Gibbet, but he that was Mr. Harrisons Servant, hanged in Chains in the same place, where that which is remaining of him may be seen to this day, but at the time of their Execution, the said Mr. Harrison was not dead, but ere seven years were over should be heard of again, yet would not confess where he was, but now it appears that the Widow Pery was a witch, and after her Sons had robd him, and cast him into a Stone Pit, she by her witch-craft conveyed him upon a Rock in the Sea near Turky, where he remained four days and nights, till a Turkish Ship coming by took him and sold him into Turky, where he remained for a season, but is now through the good providence of God returnd again safe to England, to the great wonder and admiration of all that know the same. This is undenyably true, as is sufficiently testified by Inhabitants of Cambden, and many others thereabouts.

To the Tune of Aim not too high.

Amongst those wonders which on earth are shown,
In any age there seldom hath been known,
A thing more strange than that which this Relation,
Doth here present unto your observation.

In *Glocestershire* as many know full well,
At *Cambden* Town a Gentleman did dwell,
One Mr. *William Harrison* by name,
A Stewart to a Lady of great fame.

A Widdow likewise in the Town there was,
A wicked wretch who brought strange things to pass,
So wonderful that some will scarce receive
These lines for truth nor yet my words believe.

But such as unto *Cambden* do resort,
They surely found this is no false report,
Though many lies are dayly now invented,
This is as true a Song as ere was Printed.

Therefore unto the story now give ear,
This Widow *Pery* as it doth appear,

And her two sons all fully were agreed,
Against their friend to work a wicked deed.

One of her sons even from a youth did dwell
With Mr. *Harrison* who loved him well,
And bred him up, his Mother being poor,
But see how he requited him therefore.

For taking notice that his Master went
Abroad to gather in his Ladies rent,
And by that means it was an usual thing,
For him great store of money home to bring.

He thereupon with his mischevous mother,
And likewise with his vile ungodly Brother,
Contriv'd to rob his Master, for these base
And cruel wretches were past shame and grace.

One night they met him comming into Town,
And in a barbarous manner knockt him down,
Then taking all his money quite away,
His body out of sight they did convey.

But being all suspected for this deed,
They apprehended were and sent with speed,
To *Glocester* Gaol and there upon their Tryal,
Were guilty found for all their stiff denyal.

The second part to the same Tune

It was supposed the Gentleman was dead,
And by these wretches robd and Murthered,
Therefore they were all three condem'd to death,
And eke on *Broadway-hill* they lost their breath.

One of the Sons was buried with his Mother,
Under the Gibbet, but the other Brother,
That serv'd the Gentleman, was hang'd in Chains,
And there some part of him as yet remains.

But yet before they died they did proclaim
Even in the ears of those that thither came,

That Mr. *Harrison* yet living was
And would be found in less than seven years space.

Which words of theirs for truth do now appear
For 'tis but two years since they hanged were,
And now the Gentleman alive is found
Which news is publisht through the Countrys round.

But lest that any of this truth shall doubt,
Ile tell you how the business came about.
This Widow *Pery* as tis plainly shown
Was then a Witch although it was not known.

So when these Villains by their mothers aid
Had knockt him down (even as before was said)
They took away his money every whit,
And then his body cast into a pit.

He scarce was come unto himself before
Another wonder did amaze him more,
That whilst he lookt about, he found that he
Was suddainly conveyed unto the Sea.

First on the shore he stood a little space
And thence unto a rock transported was,
Where he four days and nights did then remain
And never thought to see his friends again.

But as a Turkish ship was passing by
Some of the men the Gentleman did spy,
And took him and as I understand,
They carried him into the Turkish Land.

And there (not knowing of his sad disaster),
They quickly did provide for him a Master,
A Surgeon or of some such like profession,
Whose service he performed with much discretion.

It seems in gathering Hearbs he had good skill,
And could the same exceeding well distil,

Which to his Master great content did give,   *bloody*
And pleas'd him well so long as he did live.   *versicles*

But he soon dyd, and at his death he gave him   *107*
A piece of plate that so none should enslave him,
But that his liberty he might obtain,
To come into his native land again.

And thus this Gentleman his freedom bought,
And by a *Turky* Ship from thence was brought,
To *Portugal,* and now both safe and sound,
He is at length arrived on English ground.

Let not this seem incredible to any,
Because it is an end afirmed by many,
This is no feigned story, though tis new,
But as tis very strange tis very true.

You see how far a Witches power extends,
When as to wickedness her mind she bends,
Great is her Malice, yet can God restrain her,
And at his pleasure let her loose or chain her.

If God had let her work her utmost spight,
No doubt she would have kild the man outright,
But he is saved and she for all her malice,
Was very justly hang'd upon the Gallows.

Then let all praise to God alone be given,
By men on earth as by the Saints in heaven,
He by his mercy dayly doth befriend us,
And by his power he will still defend us.

> *London. Printed for Charles Tyus at the*
> *three Bibles on London-Bridge.*

NOTES

1. See *The Campden Wonder,* edited by Sir George Clark, Oxford University Press, 1959.
2. In *Notes and Queries,* clxxxix, 162.

Murder by Strangulation / 1

During the last half of 1895 and the first few months of the following year, the bodies of more than forty babies were found in the Thames, upriver from London; it was thought that they had died by strangulation. Then more bodies were found: one in the River Kennet and two more (in a carpet bag) in Clapper's Pool, near Reading. The body of one of the babies was wrapped in brown paper, and from this some writing was deciphered which led to the arrest of Mrs. Amelia Dyer and her son-in-law Arthur Palmer, who were running a baby farm at Caversham, Reading, charging adoption fees ranging from £10 to £100 (in terms of present-day £ purchasing power: from about £560 to about £5600). Mrs. Dyer was executed on 10 June 1896; it is recorded that Billington, the hangman, gave Mrs. Dyer a four-foot drop "to accommodate" her weight of more than fifteen stone.[1] The song, "Mrs. Dyer the Baby Farmer," was very popular at the time, and is now a favorite with audiences at the Players' Theatre, London.

> The old baby farmer has been executed;
> It's quite time she was put out of the way.
> She was a bad woman, it is not disputed;
> Not a word in her favor can anyone say.

> *Chorus*

> The old baby farmer, the wretched Mrs. Dyer,
> At the Old Bailey her wages is paid.
> In times long ago we'd have made a big fire
> And roasted so nicely that wicked old jade.

> It seems rather hard to run down a woman,
> But this one was hardly a woman at all;

To make a fine living in a way so inhuman,   *bloody*
Carousing in luxury on poor girls' downfall.   *versicles*

Poor girls who fall from the straight path of virtue,   *109*
What could they do with a child in their arms?
The fault they committed they could not undo,
So the baby was sent to the cruel baby farm.

To all these sad crimes there must be an ending;
Secrets like these for ever can't last.
Say as you like, there is no defending
The horrible tales we have heard in the past.

What did she think as she stood on the gallows,
Poor little victims in front of her eyes?
Her heart, if she had one, must have been callous;
The rope round her neck—how quickly time flies.

Down through the trap-door quickly disappearing,
The old baby farmer to eternity home,
The sound of her own death bell she was hearing.
Maybe she was sent to the cruel baby farm.

NOTE

1. According to "A Ready Reckoner for Hangmen" (appendix to *A Hand-book on Hanging* by Charles Duff, Cayme Press, 1928), a four-foot drop is dead right for a person of twelve stone.

Murder by Strangulation / 2

On Sunday morning, 22 September 1900, the body of Mary Bennett was found on the South Beach at Yarmouth; she had been criminally assaulted and strangled with a mohair boot-lace. Her scoundrel of a husband, John Herbert Bennett, was found guilty of her murder, the most damaging evidence against him being a beach photograph, taken only a few days before her death, showing her wearing a long gold chain similar to one that was discovered in his lodgings in Woolwich. Anticipating the verdict in the period between committal proceedings and trial, the following rhyme was recited:

> On the sands at Yarmouth,
> In the middle of the night,
> Poor dear Mrs. Bennett
> Was despatched without a fight.
>
> But now her killer's caught
> And he will never kill again;
> Her husband, he's the culprit,
> And they'll hang him by a chain.
>
> Just think of his audacity—
> To rape his wife before!
> There's no sufficient punishment
> In the book of English Law.

This case brought Marshall Hall, as defense counsel, into the limelight for the first time. He was convinced of Bennett's innocence, and, following the verdict, in a letter to Sir Forrest Fulton, Recorder of London, he wrote: "Personally, I cannot see any better fate for a man of that criminal nature, but that is not the question, you know very well; and I am not the sort man to worry unnecessarily about anything, least of all about a worthless man like that, but, honestly and solemnly, I do not and cannot believe that he murdered his wife."[1] Many people still question the verdict, among them Paul Capon, who suggests that the true culprit was also responsible for the murder of Dora Mary Gray, whose body was found on Yarmouth's South Beach on 14 July 1912; she, too, had been strangled with a bootlace.[2]

of the scenes outside Norwich Prison on the morning of Bennett's execution, 21 March 1901, Capon reports that "an individual with a cinematograph machine" was rivalled by a ragged ballad-seller, one of whose verses ran:

> For with the girl you had a tidy fling,
> And they found, upon my life,
> That the dead woman was your wife,
> You killed her, and now, my boy,
>   you've got to swing.

NOTES

The letter is quoted in full in *The Life of Sir Edward Marshall Hall, K.C.*, Edward Marjoribanks, Gollancz, 1930.

2. *The Great Yarmouth Mystery*, Harrap, 1965.

versicles

111

Murder by
Strangulation and Knife

On Sunday, 29 September 1935, the dismembered remains of two bodies[1] were found beneath the bridge over the stream called Gardenholme Linn, on the main road from Moffat to Edinburgh. The bodies were reconstructed by Professor James Couper Brash, Professor of Anatomy at Edinburgh University.[2] The field of inquiry was narrowed by the discovery that one of the bundles was wrapped in a special "slip" edition of the *Sunday Graphic* which was distributed only in the areas around Morecambe and Lancaster. One body was proved to be that of Isabella Van Ess, the common-law wife of Buck Ruxton, a thirty-six-year-old Parsee doctor living and practicing at 2 Dalton Square, Lancaster; the other body was that of Mary Rogerson, the nursemaid for Ruxton's children. Ruxton was tried at Manchester Assizes, and it was shown that he was insanely jealous of his wife, who he thought was having an affair with a young man in the town clerk's department of the Lancaster Corporation. The prosecution theory was adumbrated by the public in a parody of the song, "Red Sails in the Sunset":

> Red stains on the carpet,
> Red stains on your knife,
> Oh, Dr. Buck Ruxton, you cut up your wife.
> The nurse-maid, she saw you, and threatened to tell,
> So, Dr. Buck Ruxton, you killed her as well.

In examination-in-chief, Ruxton said of the first part of the theory: "That is an absolute and deliberate and fantastic story. You might as well say the sun was rising in the west and setting in the east." And of the second: "That is absolute bunkum, with a capital B, if I may say it. Why should I kill my poor Mary?" He was found guilty and hanged at Strangeways Prison, Manchester, on 12 May 1936.

There were other versions of the "Red Sails in the Sunset" parody. One of them ran:

Red stains in the bathroom,[3]
Red stains on the knife.
Oh, Dr. Buck Ruxton, you murdered your wife.
You cut her to pieces, disfigured her face,
Oh, Dr. Buck Ruxton, your name's a disgrace.

NOTES

1. Adding a touch of ghoulish fantasy, among the remains was a cyclops eye. In their introduction to the Notable British Trial volume (*Trial of Buck Ruxton*, Hodge, 1936), R. H. Blundell and G. Haswell Wilson note that the eye was better preserved than any of the other soft tissues, and suggest that "a curious possibility arises. Ruxton was known to have been interested in ophthalmology at one time and, could it have been shown that he possessed such a specimen and that it was no longer in his house, it might have formed yet another link between the bodies at Moffat and Dalton Square. In such circumstances it might have been suggested that Ruxton, in desperation to prevent the remains from declaring themselves, and being obviously unable to purchase formalin in any quantity at such a time, had sprinkled the preservative from a specimen on to the remains and had accidentally discarded the specimen itself."

These authors also quote from *The English Mail-Coach*, section 2, "The Vision of Sudden Death," by Thomas DeQuincey: "But what was Cyclops doing here? Had the medical men recommended northern air, or how? I collected, from such explanations as he volunteered, that he had an interest at stake in some suit-at-law now pending at Lancaster."

2. His work on the case, with that of Sydney Smith and John Glaister, is one of the classic achievements of the forensic sciences. See *Medico-Legal Aspects of the Ruxton Case*, Glaister and Brash, Livingstone, 1937.

3. From the *Manchester Evening News*, 14 January 1983:

The bath-tub in which Dr. Buck Ruxton chopped up his common-law wife and his nursemaid still survives—as a drinking trough for police horses. . . . Few know that the white enamel tub—Exhibit "A" at the sensational trial at the Manchester Assize Court, Strangeways—is now at the police stables at Longton, near Preston. The tub spent many years in the "black museum" of the forensic laboratories at Lancashire

Constabulary headquarters at Preston before being moved to Long-
ton. It carries a brass plaque:

"This bath was used by Dr. Buck Ruxton when mutilating
the bodies of his wife and his maid on an unknown date be-
tween the 14th and the 29th September, 1935, at 2 Dalton Square,
Lancaster."

Murder by Strangulation / 3

On 2 December 1949, acting on information contained in a series of contradictory statements made by Timothy John Evans, an illiterate van driver, the police searched 10 Rillington Place,[1] Notting Hill Gate, and found the bodies of Evans's wife Beryl and their one-year-old daughter Geraldine; both had been strangled, the woman with a rope or twisted nylon stocking, the baby with a necktie. Indicted for the murder of the baby, Evans was found guilty, and was executed on 5 March 1950. One of the leading prosecution witnesses at the trial was John Reginald Halliday Christie, an ex–War Reserve policeman, who was the tenant of the ground-floor flat at 10 Rillington Place. Three years later, the remains of six more women were found in the house and garden. One of them was Christie's wife Ethel, and it was for her murder that he was tried and found guilty.[2] Not only did Christie admit responsibility for the deaths of the other five women, but he gave detailed evidence purporting to show that he had murdered Beryl Evans; he denied, however, that he had killed the baby. John Scott Henderson, a Queen's Counsel, was appointed by the home secretary to inquire into the evidence and report whether, in his opinion, there had been a miscarriage of justice in the Evans case. After hearing, in private, the evidence of twenty-three persons, one of whom was Christie (who was hanged a few days later, on 15 July 1953), Scott Henderson stated, amongst other findings, that there was no doubt that Evans was responsible for the deaths of his wife and baby.[3] But few people were satisfied, either with the way in which the inquiry had been conducted or with the

findings, and in 1957 Ewan MacColl epitomized their feelings
about the case in his song, "Go Down, You Murderers":[4]

Tim Evans was a prisoner fast in his prison cell,
And those who read about his crimes, they damned his soul to
  hell,
(*Chorus*) Saying, "Go down, you murderer, go down!"

For the murder of his own dear wife and the killing of his
  child,
The jury found him guilty and the hanging judge he smiled,
(*Chorus*)

Evans pleaded innocent and he swore by Him on high,
That he never killed his own dear wife nor caused his child to
  die,
(*Chorus*)

So they moved him out of "C" block to his final flowery dell,
And day and night two screws were there, and they never left
  his cell,
(*Chorus*)

Sometimes they played draughts with him and solo and pon-
  toon,
To stop him brooding on the rope that was to be his doom,
(*Chorus*)

They brought his grub in on a tray, there were eggs and meat
  and ham,
And all the snout that he could smoke was there at his com-
  mand,
(*Chorus*)

Evans walked in the prison yard and the screws they walked
  behind,
And he saw the sky above the wall but he knew no peace of
  mind,
(*Chorus*)

They came for him at eight o'clock and the chaplain read a
  prayer,
And then they walked him to that place where the hangman
  did prepare,
  (*Chorus*)

The rope was fixed around his neck and a washer behind his
  ear,
And the prison bell was tolling, but Tim Evans did not hear,
  (*Chorus*)

A thousand lags were cursing and a-banging on the doors,
Tim Evans did not hear them, he was deaf for evermore,
  (*Chorus*)

They sent Tim Evans to the drop for a crime he didn't do,
It was Christie was the murderer, and the judge and jury too,
Saying, "Go down, you murderers, go down!"

In 1965, mainly due to the efforts of a group that included
Ludovic Kennedy[5] and Evans's mother, Mr. Justice Brabin
was appointed to hold a public inquiry, and in October 1966,
his report was published, with the findings: "I have come to
the conclusion that it is more probable than not that Evans
killed Beryl Evans. I have come to the conclusion that it is
more probable than not that Evans did not kill Geraldine."[6]

The who-killed-whom? controversy continues. But far too
many of the people who assert that Evans was completely in-
nocent of murder rely upon the element of coincidence, say-
ing that it is impossible to believe that two men, independent
of each other, would commit murder in the same house. This
is a pink herring; such a coincidence *could* occur. In the base-
ment of 13 Finborough Road, which is in the same London
borough as Notting Hill Gate, Ronald True murdered a pros-
titute named Olive Young; only two doors away, at No. 17,
George Epton murdered a Piccadilly pick-up girl named Win-
ifred Mulholland. (And there is a proper, though not quite
relevant, coincidence: an upstairs room of No. 13 was the
home and business location of Robert Wood's lady-friend.)

1. Subsequently renamed Ruston Close, it is now called Ruston *Mews.*

2. See *Trials of Evans and Christie* (Hodge, 1953). F. Tennyson Jesse, the editor of this volume in the "Notable British Trials" series, privately referred to the cases as "The Feast of Corpses Christie."

3. *Report of an inquiry into certain matters arising out of the deaths of Mrs. Beryl Evans and of Geraldine Evans and out of the conviction of Timothy John Evans of the murder of Geraldine Evans,* Cmd 8946, Her Majesty's Stationery Office (hereafter HMSO), 1953.

4. Recorded on *Chorus from the Gallows,* Topic, 12T16.

5. Author of *Ten Rillington Place,* Gollancz, 1961.

6. *The Case of Timothy John Evans, Report of an Inquiry by The Hon. Mr. Justice Brabin,* CMd 3101, HMSO, 1966. Following the publication of the Brabin report, Robert F. Hussey, the American crime historian, wrote to me:

> The entire matter of re-opening that farcical Scott Henderson inquiry is most gratifying. I had begun to think that future *Iolanthe* performances would have to feature a fatter Martyn Green (now a Home Secretary) singing:

> > The Law is the true embodiment
> > Of everything that's excellent.
> > It has no kind of fault or flaw,
> > For Scott, and I, embody the Law.

Murder by Strangulation, Improvised Blackjack, and Ice-pick

In November 1938, a New York jury found Robert Irwin, a twenty-eight-year-old sculptor, guilty of triple-murder, and he was sentenced to 139 years in prison. Within ten days of his arrival at Sing Sing, the prison doctors found him to be psychotic, and he was transferred to a hospital for the criminally insane. No one was very surprised. Samuel Leibowitz, Irwin's defense counsel, had called him "completely crazy" and said that his brain was "like a scrambled egg."

The psychiatric evidence prompted the following verse from a Hearst columnist:

> *It's All Done by Mirrors!*
>
> He did not murder anyone
> And such a charge not nice is:
> He's just the charming victim of
> A "catathymic crisis."[1]

NOTE

1. Quoted by Frederick Wertham in *The Show of Violence*, Gollancz, 1949.

Murder by Suffocation / 1

Those enterprising partners in multicide, Burke and Hare (both called William, and both born in Ireland), who, in 1828, provided Dr. Robert Knox with a plentiful supply of suffocated specimens for his dissecting table at 10 Surgeons' Square, Edinburgh, were the subject of many chapbook and broadsheet verses, of which the best-known is

> Up the close and doun the stair,
> But and ben¹ with Burke and Hare;
> Burke's the butcher, Hare's the thief,
> Knox the boy that buys the beef.

Their noxious but lucrative trade (average price for a "subject," £10 in winter, £8 in summer) came to an end on Saturday, 1 November 1828, when a beggar couple lodging with Burke discovered a body beneath some straw at the foot of a bed; by the time a policeman arrived, the body had been removed to Dr. Knox's, but sufficient evidence was obtained to take Burke and his mistress, Helen M'Dougal, into custody, and to arrest Mr. and Mrs. Hare later in the day. The authorities, faced with a "some-or-none" legal problem, had no difficulty in persuading Hare to turn king's evidence, and at 9:30 A.M. on Christmas Eve, Burke and Helen M'Dougal were placed at the bar in the Justiciary Court House in Parliament Square; the chief prosecution witnesses were Hare and his wife (who throughout the trial carried a baby suffering from whooping cough, "whose every paroxysm seemed to fire her with intenser anger and impatience"). Almost exactly twenty-four hours later, on Christmas morning, Burke was pro-
nounced guilty. Due only to the masterly advocacy of her

William Burke. "*Drawn from Life in the Lock-up House on the day before his Execution by his own consent,*" *by Benjamin W. Crombie*

counsel, Henry Cockburn, the jury found that the case against Helen M'Dougal was not proven. Burke, quite calm, turned to his mistress and said, "Nelly, you are out of the scrape." He was hanged on 28 January 1829; when the body had been cut down—and long before it had been carted away—the hangman's assistants sold pieces of the rope at half-a-crown an inch.

> 'Midst a fiendish yell, Burke danced to hell;
> 'Gainst him the door old Satan locks.
> Says he, this place you shan't disgrace;
> Go back to earth and dwell with Knox!

The execution is wonderfully described by William Bolitho:[2]

> At eight o'clock our poor jackal was brought out for his ordained end, which was accomplished within a quarter of an hour, with all the educative ritual of public execution: the great shout; the muffling; the slight hitch, caused by the nerves of the stage-frightened hangman, the last prayer and signal; the silence, the drop. The undertaker's men gave his feet a twirl. Burke, like a big curiously-shaped top, spun out into the air and out of life. His body, with platitudinous aptness, was taken for dissection, not to the broken-windowed establishment of his old patron, but to the rival theatre of Doctor Monro, where it was shown to all fashionable Edinburgh, to the great good of the house.[3]

Sir Walter Scott, who had a reserved seat at the execution, recorded in his journal:

> Burke the murderer hanged this morning. The mob, which was immense, demanded Knox and Hare, but, though greedy for more victims, received with shouts the solitary wretch who found his way to the gallows out of five or six who seem not less guilty than he.

Dr. Knox (who was known to his students as "Old Cyclops"—an attack of smallpox had atrophied his left eye, leaving only the socket) was regarded by the people of Edinburgh

in an even worse light than Burke and Hare; "he was gener-
ally held to be not only their partner, but their patron and the
instigator of their crimes, possibly even their instructor in the
art of 'burking'. "[4] One broadsheet ballad, entitled "A Timely
Hint to Anatomical Practitioners" and headed with a portrait
of Knox, contained the lines:

> Men, women, children, old and young,
>   The sickly and the hale,
> Were murdered, packed up, and sent off
>   To K———'s human sale.

> That man of skill, with subjects warm,
>   Was frequently supplied,
> Nor did he question when or how
>   The person brought had died.

It is impossible to say how many corpses were produced by
Burke and Hare; sixteen seems to be the minimum number.
Certainly there were many more than are mentioned in the
following account, which provides little more than a cross sec-
tion of their crimes:

The Recent Murders

> God prosper long our noble King,
> Our lives and safeties all,
> I'll sing of murders that till now
> Did never yet befall.

> In modern Athens, as it's called,
> In Western Portsburgh Street,
> Two murderers had their horrid den,
> And there did nightly meet.

> These wretches' names were Burke and Hare,
> Both from the sister Isle;
> Their plan was to take strangers in
> And them of life beguile.

> Which having done, they wrapped them up
> And laid them in a box,

And without either dread or fear,
Sold them to Dr. K——.

The first was Margaret Paterson,
Whom drink had led astray;
She fell into their wicked hands,
Who choked her as she lay.

Next on the list was daft Jamie,
Who laughed and sang sae crouse,
And seeking his mother was decoyed
Into the murderers' house.

Next was the wife who came to town
In search of her dear son,
Was by these wicked wretches dogged
And barbarously undone.

Last, Burke had seized an infant dear,
Oh! horrible disgrace,
Who while he choked it on his knee
Did smile up in his face.

Such are the horrid deeds of Burke,
Deeds never done before,
Who since his sentence has confessed
To twenty murders more.

His trusty friend, the wicked Hare,
Now waits alike his fate,
And though vengeance is often slow,
It never comes too late.

Now all ye powers that rule above,
Grant we may evil shun,
And that henceforth such dreadful acts
May never more be done.

The murder which roused the greatest public indignation
was that of James Wilson (the "daft Jamie" of the sixth verse);
a feebleminded but kindhearted boy of eighteen who earned

a few pennies by running errands and doing light casual work, he was a well-known character in the Old Town of Edinburgh.

He's to be pitied, that's such a silly elf,
Who cannot speak nor wrestle for himself.
Jamie was such a simpleton
He'd not fight with a boy.
Nor did he ever curse or swear
At those who'd him annoy.

Edinburgh's only memorial to Burke and Hare is a public house named after them which stands almost opposite the site of their crimes in the West Port. Vamped from the old "Main Point Bar," "The Burke and Hare" was opened in the summer of 1969. The interior is like a psychedelic space capsule; there are a few naive wall paintings, and behind the bar are modern portraits, quite pretty but hardly lifelike, of the murderers.[5]

Until recently—perhaps still—Edinburgh's children's skipping-chant repertoire included:

Burke an' Hare
Fell doun the stair,
Wi' a body in a box
Gaun to Doctor Knox.

NOTES

1. Out and in.
2. "The Science of William Burke," *Murder for Profit*, Dobson, 1953.
3. The skeleton now hangs in the Anatomical Museum of Edinburgh University.
4. *Knox the Anatomist*, Isobel Rae, Oliver & Boyd, 1964.
5. So now Edinburgh has two criminous inns: "Deacon Brodie's Tavern" in the Lawnmarket (where Burke was hanged) is named after the man whose double life—respectable by day, criminal by night—inspired Stevenson to write *Dr. Jekyll and Mr. Hyde*. Brodie was hanged for theft in 1788 on gallows which he himself had designed.

Murder by Suffocation / 2

Burke and Hare started a homicidal fashion, and from 1829 to 1832, when the Anatomy Act diminished the demand, many persons were arrested for "burking." One of these was Eliza Ross, who, in the Solomon Grundy–like style of the times, was tried on Friday (6 January 1832) and died on Monday (the 9th) for the murder of an eighty-four-year-old woman called Elizabeth Walsh. The main witness at the trial of Eliza Ross and her husband, accused with her, was their twelve-year-old son. The following is condensed from a broadsheet:

> The Court opened at an early hour, and Mr. Adolphus opened the case.
>
> The prisoner Ross exclaimed to her son as she was being forwarded to the dock, "Do not tell no lies to hang your father and mother."
>
> Edward Cook, son of the prisoners, examined—I recollect the old lady, Elizabeth Walsh, coming to the house, 7 Goodman's Yard, Minories. In the evening the old lady, my mother and myself had some coffee for supper. It made me, and also the old lady, sleepy, and she shortly afterwards stretched herself on my father and mother's bed. Some time after, I saw my mother go the bedside and place her right hand over the mouth of the old lady, and her left over her body. My mother continued in this position for upwards of half an hour. The old woman did not struggle, but her eyes stared and rolled very much. I stood by the fire, and my father during the whole transaction was looking out at the window, and I am positive he did not turn round once to see what was going on. [The next day] I went to school. On returning

home, I found my father beating my mother, and thought the cause to be that the latter had been drinking with the grand-daughter of the old lady, who had called to enquire after her. We all supped together, and at ten o'clock my mother left the room, and while standing at the window I saw her go by with a sack on her shoulder. The next morning my mother told me she had taken the body to the London Hospital.

The jury, after retiring for a quarter of an hour, returned a verdict of Guilty Death against Ross, and acquitted her husband, but detained him on another indictment.

The account of the execution is reproduced verbatim:

Early in the morning, an unusual number of females were assembled to witness the termination of the unhappy Culprit, who after joining with Mr. Cotton, the Minister of Newgate, a few minutes in prayer, the hangman then continued his duty, and she expeated her crimes in this world without any apparent struggle. The croud was emence.

Mr. Quick of Bowling Green Lane, the printer of the broadsheet, gave good value for money. As well as the account of the trial and of the execution, he reproduced two drawings, and finished up with some verses:

The Sorrowful Lamentations
and Last Farewell to the World
of Eliza Ross

Behold a wretched woman base,
Who was confined in Newgate cell,
The feelings of her guilty heart
No person with a tongue can tell.

On Friday at the bar she stood,
It would make your very blood run cold
To see her child against her swear,
A little boy scarce twelve years old.

He swore his mother did commit
Before his eyes that cruel deed;
To hear him give his evidence
Caused eyes to weep and hearts to bleed.

The judge declared she guilty was,
And for her crimes was doomed to die
On Monday last, to public gaze
Exposed, upon the gallows high.

She was tried and cast, her sentence past,
And all her weeping was in vain.
In this world below, her time is short,
And she will never Burke again.[1]

A poor old aged woman dear,
This wretch to murder did engage,
And on her bed did strangle her,
Full eighty-four years was her age.

Now Justice has her overtook,
In Newgate she did weep forlorn,
Her crimes have brought her to the tree,
And she has died a death of scorn.

NOTE

1. So far as I know, William Burke is the only murderer who has contributed to the English dictionary: *burke*, *vt* to murder, esp. by stifling: hence (*fig*) to put an end to quietly.

Murder by Truncheon

The initial hostility to the "new police" (the Peelers), formed in 1829, was reflected in, and probably increased by, the broadsheets of the time. Even quite trivial transgressions by members of the force (constable's wage: 19 shillings a week) were reported and made the subject of ballads. In 1830 the broadsheet vendors really had something to shout about:

> Saturday the neighborhood of Shadwell and Wapping was in a state of excitement owing to a report which had gained circulation that a waterman named John Peacock Wood, residing in Lower Shadwell, had been MUR-DERED by the New Police. It appears that on Thursday night at 12 o'clock, whilst in a state of intoxication, he was removed from the White Hart public house in Shadwell High Street, and was thrown from the door into the street by a policeman. He lay on the ground for some time, when the inspector of the K Division directed several policemen to take him to the station house. This was accordingly done, but on the way thither he met with some further ill-usage from the policemen, who were seen to throw him down, and afterwards to search him, and take some money from him in the street. He was locked up in one of the cells in the station house at Green Bank, Wapping, where he continued all night in a state of insensibility.
>
> On Friday morning he appeared in a dying condition and was removed to his own house, and expired the same afternoon. Yesterday morning a post-mortem examination of the body took place. Under the direction of Mr. Millard, a demonstrator of anatomy, it was found that the skull was fractured, and he had received other

injuries to his head inflicted by a truncheon or some round instrument, which had caused his death.

Mary Ford stated at the Coroner's Inquest that she was an unfortunate woman. She met the deceased at the White Hart on Thursday night, and after having some gin and beer they were going home, when two police-men came in for the purpose of clearing the house and told them to go. John Douglas, 279K, seized Wood by the shoulder and dragged him to the door, and soon as it was open, he was thrown with great force into the street and fell on the curb stone.

Several witnesses deposed to the violence which the deceased had received from six policemen. It is evident that the man's skull was not fractured when the police entered the White Hart.

Coroner: How did Douglas shove him out?

Witness: He shoved him right out in the street. The deceased did not resist.

Coroner: Was there more force used than necessary?

Witness: I can't say what was necessary but Douglas handled him very roughly. . . . The deceased was taken into the station house on the back of a coal whipper. There were 5 or 6 policemen with him. Having laid him down on the ground, they dragged him towards the cell with his head trailing on the ground. (A dead murmur of horror here marked the proceedings.)

When this went to Press the reporter has made no return at present.

'Tis of a Dreadful Deed of Blood
To you I will unfold,
The slaughter of a waterman;
'Twill make your blood run cold.
On Thursday eve at Ratcliffe Highway
At the White Hart he drank so free,
But little did he think that night
Would prove his destiny.

The Policemen came into the house
The people for to clear;

Seeing John Wood intoxicated,
To him they were severe.
They dragged him over to the door
Without any fear or dread.
On the stones there he was dashed
And with the Truncheon they split his head.

After they had ill-used this man
With their arbitrary power,
They dragged him to the station house,
They were above an hour.
O, had you but heard his moans,
Would have grieved your heart full sore.
When they took him to the station
He lyed weltering on the floor.

Then to had to the Cruelty,
Most dreadful for to tell,
All in his Crimson Gore
He was Confined in a Dismal Cell.
No surgical assistance for him they got
Until the next day,
But then, alas! it was too late,
Death had summoned him away.

The Skull before the Inquest was brought
And on the table placed,
While Grief and Consternation
Was painted on each face.
The Policemen must answer for this crime
All on a future day,
For the killing of a Waterman
In Ratcliffe Highway.[1]

NOTE

1. It appears that no legal action was taken against any of the allegedly overzealous policemen.

Attempted Murder
by Strangulation

On 30 June 1829, Ann Chapman, who was twenty-eight, was hanged for attempting to strangle her three-weeks-old baby at Acton, now well within the bounds of Greater London but then quite rural in Middlesex. The verse is taken from a broadsheet.

> Now mothers all, whose tender hearts
> Doat on your infants dear,
> Think of Ann Chapman's cruel act,
> And shed a pitying tear;
> With no compassion in her heart,
> Even when her infant smil'd,
> She with a cord did rashly aim
> To strangle her dear child.
>
> She left it in a ditch to die,
> Where chance no one might lead,
> But Providence, with watchful eye,
> Revealed the cruel deed.
> The infant sav'd—from the intent
> A public death to prove,
> She warns all women who forget
> A tender mother's love.

Adultery

Attempted Suicide

Bigamy

Delinquency

Fraudulent Conversion

Incest

Adultery

In 1886 Lord Colin Campbell, youngest son of the Duke of Argyll, sued his wife for divorce on the grounds of her adultery with the Duke of Marlborough; Captain Shaw,[1] Chief of the Metropolitan Fire Brigade; Mr. Bird, a doctor who had professionally attended her; and General Butler. Cross-petitioning, Lady Campbell accused her husband of adultery with a housemaid called Amelia Watson. In support of Lady Campbell's petition, Lady Miles, her cousin, claimed that she had caught Lord Colin and Amelia Watson in *flagrante delicto;* but Dr. Clement Godson, an eminent authority called for the defense, said that he had examined the housemaid and found her *virgo intacta.* His evidence inspired the rhyme:

> Amelia Watson is my name,
> And housemaid is my station;
> *Virgo intacta* I'm proclaimed,
> And Godson's my salvation.

The jury returned a verdict for the respondent in each case. No adultery had been proved.

NOTE

1. From *Iolanthe* (first performed in 1882):

> Oh, Captain Shaw,
> Type of true love kept under!
> Could thy Brigade
> With cold cascade
> Quench my great love, I wonder?

Attempted Suicide

The Suicide Act 1961 . . . abrogated the law whereby it was a crime for a person to commit suicide. In consequence, attempted suicide ceased to be a misdemeanor. The Act made it a criminal offense to aid, abet, counsel, or procure the suicide of another person, thus allaying the fears of those who thought that the repeal of the old law would encourage suicide pacts.

Shortly after the passing of the Suicide Act the Ministry of Health in London issued a memorandum advising all doctors and authorities concerned that attempted suicide was to be regarded as a medical and social problem and that every such case ought to be seen by a psychiatrist. This attitude to suicide is much more in keeping with present-day knowledge and sentiment than the purely moralistic and punitive reaction expressed in the old law.

Erwin Stengel,
Suicide and Attempted Suicide,
Penguin, 1964.

Epigram

When would-be Suicides in purpose fail—
Who could not find a morsel though they needed—
If Peter sends them for attempts to jail,
What would he do to them if they succeeded?

Thomas Hood

Bigamy

On 15 April 1776, Elizabeth Chudleigh, for twenty-five years a Maid of Honor to the Princess of Wales, was tried for bigamy by the House of Lords, the charge being that she had married the Duke of Kingston while still the wife of the Earl of Bristol. Found guilty, she claimed the privilege of peerage, and, after a long legal argument, was discharged.

In Westminster the broadsheet sellers had a field day with:

> There was a maid—
> A Maid of Honor,
> And strange, 'tis said
> Of this strange maid,
> She was no maid,
> She had no honor.

Delinquency / 1

The Life of a Cadger
A Favorite Characteristic Medley Song
Tune: "The Knife Grinder"

I am a knowing cadger as ever tramp'd the town,
As ever cadg'd a penny, or yarnt a honest brown.
Vhile I'm travelling the East, Sal's travelling in the Vest,
And out and out ve manages to feather *hour* nest.

Tune: "Luddy Fuddy"

On Monday I chalks my mug so neat,
Luddy fuddy, right fol luddy, I oh—
And shams a strong fit in the street,
But the tin soon fetches me on my feet,
Luddy fuddy, right fol lar a luddy, I oh!

SPOKEN: Yes, but I knows wot brings me round sooner
nor all—that's the sight of a *Robert.* I always puts a bit of
soap in my mouth, to give the fit more effect, like.
T'other day, vhile I vos kicking about on all fours, up
comed a Peeler. How are yer off for soap? says he. Vot's
that to you? says I. Vhen he crammed his leg o'mutton
fist in my mouth, and boned the piece of mottled. For
that artful dodge I got a month on the *Brixton Railvay,* to
dance the *Poker.* But I knows vot brings me round sooner
nor all—that's a bucket of cold vater flung over me, like
they sarves pugnacious hanimals in the dog days, vhen
they've got the *highdryfubby*—it's an out and out *cold vater
cure.* [1]

Chorus
Tune: "Drops of Brandy"

Then upon me in pity look down—
I'm hunted about like a badger:

Tip me a bob or a brown,
Vhile I sings you the life of a cadger.

Tune: "All round my Hat"

All round the squares, and round about the *aireys,*
All round the squares, on a quiet afternoon:
And vhen the flunkies turn their backs, I comes the
   presto business,
And takes the unkimmon care, too, of all their silver
   spoons.
All round the squares Sal lugs a pair of babbies—
All round the squares Sal lugs a pair of twins:
And vhen the public passes by, she pinches 'em
   woraciously,
Vhich makes the babbies for a cry, and sympathy it vins.

SPOKEN: Yes, but that babby caper ain't all profit, nei-
ther. Ve has to pay five bob a day for the hire of them ere
kids—and vhen they grows too big, ve has to change 'em
for a couple a size or two less. T'other day, vhile my old
woman vos out, up cum'd an old lady—(a hout and hout
customer—never tipt her less than a Joey, except on ban
yan days, then she'd drop her tuppence)—so she says to
my Sarah, How is it, mum, that your children never
grows no bigger? Howsumdever she's always vide-o—
catch a veazel asleep and shave his vhiskers—so she
says—the fact on it is, marm, the kids is hobstinate, and
von't grow. Von't grow, said the old lady, vhy vot d'ye
mean by that? Vhy, says Sarah, they're so werry lazy they
vants to be carried—so they've made up their minds not
to grow not no biggerer. That vos a regular extinguisher
for her, and no flies!
             Then upon, etc.

Tune: "Irish Molly, O"

Vhen the rain's a pelting down, half naked out I go,
And I larns the art of shivering, vhile the stormy vinds
   do blow,
The flats they pull their vinders up, the browns all out
   to throw,
And if they're bobs or sixpences, I arn't offended—no!

Tune: "The Long Letter"

Then I flings my corpse into the river,
Vhere there's plenty to drag me *safe* on shore—
Sal comes up, a long tale to deliver,
To say I've been out of vurk six months or more.
Tears from the people's eyes are flowing—
Ten or twelve bob they gathers me soon,
Then off ve goes, vith a vink so knowing,
And gets jolly drunk at the Man in the Moon.

SPOKEN: Then ve fakes up the starved out Manchester
chizzle. Myself, Sarah, and the kids—ve turns out of a
morning with clean mugs, and myself vith a vhite apron
in front of me, and I pitches 'em a yarn in this style, af-
ter the manner of Mister A. Smith. Ladies and genteel-
men—It is with most painful feelings of regret I appear
before you—but necessity is the mother of invention.
You see before you not the substance but the shadow of
an unfortunate cotton spinner, therefore you will par-
don me if I pitch you a long *yarn*—but the *thread* of my
discourse is *spun* out in a few words, without getting you
in a *line.* I have been out of work this eight-and-thirty
years, and my wife here will tell you the same. Open
therefore your philanthropic and preposterous hearts,
and don't allow parsimonious feelings to predominate
till I pre-occupy the little present which I had a presen-
timent that you would present me with. We are without
the common necessaries of life, and it is quite necessary
you should know it. We have none of us tasted sucking
pig for this last fortnight—and as to roast fowl, it's a
stranger to us. Bestow a few rags to cover the nakedness
of our two blessed kids. Some of your left-off satin
dresses would meet with our approbation—and my
wife, who is as "all ladies wish to be who love their
lords," would likewise be happy to accept of all the babby
linen your charitable and benevolent bosums might feel
disposed to shower down upon her. As to myself, I am
content with little. As the poet says—"Man wants but lit-
tle here below, nor wants that little long." Give me but a

suit of clothes—a pair of Wellington boots, and one of
your best beaver hats, and your petitioners will ever
pray for—

Tune: "Street Chaunt"

We've got no work to do-o-o—we've got no work to do-o-o!
We're all the way from Manchester, and we *wants no work*
to do.

Tune: "Fim along Fosey"

Sometimes I goes out vith my arm tied in a sling—
Sal goes out vith ballads, and chaunts the "Bridal Ring."
Sometimes I goes out vith my face tied up in rags—
Sal sneaks about the linen-drapers', looking arter swags.
Sometimes I blacks up my mug, and sweeps crossings like
   a nigger,
Sal goes to the artists', and lets out her crummy *figger*—
But the best of all bisnesses I've not mentioned yet,
Is the begging letter caper, and tidy sums ve get.

SPOKEN: Yes—if I hadn't a larnt the art of penmanship
'twould have been mix'd pickles vith us long ago. The
suicide dodge gets too common nowadays—folks does it
in ernest—and the starved out caper is a case of cold
coffee—so we sets down and writes billy duchxes. I
wrote for Sal to Queen Addlegg, saying she was a poor
widder with eighteen kids—no father—mouths full of
emptiness, and not nothink to put in 'em. The result of
that tender appeal was a yellow boy. Long live her dow-
agership! says I. Then I penned one to the *Duk* of Well-
ington, saying as how I was a old soldier—lost both my
eyes at Sallymanka, both my arms at Bunker's Hill, and
both my legs at Waterloo—so I vos regerly *stumped,* and
only depended upon his stumpy. The Duk, werry much
infected, sent me down a fourpenny bit, and asked me to
call some day when he was *out.* No—sooner than I'd
stoop to a Joey, I'd drive a cab on the Thames, or bail
out the sea with a mustard spoon!
         Then upon me, etc.

                    JOHN LABERN,
         Labern's Funny Song Book, 1852

Brown = copper coin; the tin, Robert, Peeler = policeman; Joey = three-penny piece; banyan days = days of short commons; yellow boy = sovereign; stumpy = money.

NOTE

1. The cold-water cure (hydrotherapy) achieved great popularity in the middle years of the nineteenth century. Two of its leading practitioners—Dr. James Manby Gully (see page 83) and Dr. Thomas Smethurst—were involved in controversial poisoning cases.

Delinquency / 2

The Chickaleary Cove[1]

I'm a Chickaleary bloke with my one, two, three,
Whitechapel was the village I was born in,
For to get me on the hop, or on my tibby drop,
You must wake up very early in the morning.
I have a rorty gal, also a knowing pal,
And merrily together we jog on,
I doesn't care a flatch, as long as I've a tach,
Some pannum for my chest, and a tog on.

Now kool my downy kicksies—the style for me,
Built on a plan werry naughty,
The stock around my squeeze a guiver color see,
And the vestat with the bins so rorty.
My tailor sews you well, from a perger to a swell,
At Groves' you are safe to make a sure pitch,
For ready yenom down, there ain't a shop in town,
Can lick Groves in the Cut as well as Shoreditch.

Off to Paris I shall go, to show a thing or two
To the dipping blokes what hangs about the caffes,
How to do a cross-fam, for a super, or a slang,
And to bustle them grand'armes I'd give the office:
Now, my pals, I'm going to slope, see you soon again, I hope,
My young woman is avaiting, so be quick,
Now join in a chyike, the jolly we all like.
I'm off with a party to the "Vic."

Chickaleary cove (or bloke) = artful fellow; tibby = head; rorty = smart;
flatch = bad half-crown; tach = hat; pannum = food; tog = garment; kick-
sies = breeches; squeeze = silk; guiver = flash, smart; vestat = waist-coat;
bins = pockets; yenom = money (back slang); dipping blokes = pick-

pockets; cross-fam = a method of picking pockets; super = watch; slang = watch-chain; bustle = dupe; office = information; slope = leave; chyike = shout; jolly = sham fight for the purpose of drawing a crowd of people, whose pockets can then be picked.

NOTE

1. Composed and sung by the "Great" Vance during the 1860s.

Delinquency / 3

Blooming Aesthetic

HE

A dealer-in-coke young man,
A wallop-his-moke young man,
A slosher-of-pals,
A spooning-with-gals,
An ought-to-be-blowed young man.

A tell-a-good-whopper young man,
A slogging-a-copper young man,
A pay-on-the-nod,
An always-in-quod,
A sure-to-be-scragged young man.

A Sunday-flash-togs young man,
A pocket-of-hogs young man,
A save-all-his-rhino,
A cut-a-big-shine, oh,
Will soon-have-a-pub young man.

SHE

A powder-and-paint young girl,
Not-quite-a-saint young girl,
An always-get-tight,
A stay-out-all-night,
Have-a-kid-in-the-end young girl.

Make-a-bloke-choke young girl,
Love-a-gin-soak young girl,
On-the-kerb-come-a-cropper,
Run-in-by-a-copper,
"Fined-forty-bob"—young girl.

A tallow-faced-straight young girl,
A never-out-late young girl,

A Salvation-mummery,
Smoleless-and-glummery,
Kid-by-a-captain young girl.

ANON, *The Rag*, 1882

Fraudulent Conversion

Towards the end of his biography of Horatio Bottomley,[1] Julian Symons writes:

> Bottomley seems a series of public attitudes rather than a person. The company promoter, bland and smiling, triumphing over angry shareholders; the well-paid recruiting agent, arms outspread, tears in his eyes; the lay lawyer yearning with sincerity; the Cockney wit and champagne guzzler. All this blended to make a wonderfully rich public personality, but behind the public personality there was, in any serious sense, no character at all. . . . He needed to prove . . . that the greatest lay lawyer in England was above the law; and throughout his life the plans he made for hoodwinking shareholders and accountants were in some ways skilful and subtle and in other ways remarkably careless. It was necessary for him to place difficulties in his own way so that he might overcome them. Probably the most important moments in his life were those in which he was able to triumph over awkward questions about the failure to publish accounts with such answers as: "He was appealed to by Mr. Snow as to where the £700,000 had gone. He could only say, in all sincerity and honesty, he had not the remotest idea." To succeed by pure audacity through the skill of his own tongue in defiance of logic or figures—that was what he valued.

In May 1922, Bottomley discovered that there was truth in the saying that a man who defends himself has a fool for a client. He was found guilty of fraudulent conversion and sentenced to seven years' imprisonment. Earning remission, he was released after just over five years, and soon afterwards published a collection of verses written during his stay in prison.[2] To ensure that no one missed what to him seemed a clear parallel between himself and Wilde, he persuaded Lord Alfred Douglas to write a foreword to the book.

The flavor of the longest work, "Convict '13' (A Ballad of Maidstone Gaol),"[3] is conveyed in these excerpts:

> His daily comrades murderers
> And cut-throats by the score;
> Receivers, forgers, traffickers,
> And burglars, too, galore;
> Incendiaries and perjurers,
> Garrotters, thieves, and spies,
> Blackmailers, pimps, and procurers—
> The list the pen defies!
> Abandoned youth, already old,
> With men of evil fame,
> Who talk (ah, God! and more than talk!)
> Of deeds of sin and shame;
> Defying Nature's barriers
> For purity of Life—
>
> A sister's, daughter's sanctity,
> Or chastity of wife:
> The vile depraved degenerate
> Of every type and vogue;
> The wife deserter, bigamist,
> Sex roué, rake, and rogue,
> E'en lunatics and idiots—
> The halt, the maim, the blind;
> The epileptic, paralyzed—
> Life's wrecks of every kind . . . .
>
> At exercise on asphalt path,
> Around—around—around—
> In silent march, funereal,
> With eyes upon the ground,
> He hears the muttered oath and curse,
> The whispered plan and threat,

And wonders, as he counts the days,
Does God at times forget?

The following verses are chosen simply as a cross section of
Bottomley's moods and styles.

Horatio III!

In classic lore of Roman days
(Apart from Lord Macauley's "Lays")
We read of three *Horatii*
Who fought the *Curiatii*.
And now in modern times we see
Three more Horatios of degree—
Lord Nelson, Kitchener—and *me!*

☛

A High Court Doggerel
(Without Rhyme, Reason or Rhythm)

I wonder if you've ever thought
The Law Courts being High
Explains a lot of little things—
Er—*ex hypothesi.*
It first of all should make quite clear
Why law is such a failure,
The Judges living in the clouds—
Of course that's *inter alia.*
And why they give themselves such airs,
With eyes turned towards the sky,
Of wit and wisdom from above—
And that's *a fortiori.*
Another thing it should make clear:
Why precedents they bandy,
Sometimes before your case begins,
About your *locus standi.*
A few things now to bear in mind
The other side to floor 'em:
That first, when pricing up a thing,
To charge it *ad valorem.*

And then, upon the other hand,
Your creditor to hit,
Demand before you pay a cent
A *quantum meruit*.
And setting off against a debt
How far you can and can't go,
The rule of law to recollect
Is credit it *pro tanto*.
Another point to keep in mind—
You'll find it come in handy—
That every item he must prove:
The onus is *probandi*.
And finally I would impress
That when you've won the day,
Instruct your lawyer there and then,
Take out a writ of *fi. fa.*

With these things and a little luck
You'll leave the blessed shanty
To find that, when you've paid the costs,
The status is *quo ante*.

But do not be at all dismayed—
The law was sent to "try" us,
In Chancery or Session House,
Or King's Bench *nisi prius*.
So give three cheers for British Law,
Your troubles it will heal 'em;
No need its motto to repeat—
It ends with *ruat coelum*.

Of course there is a certain sense
In which the Courts are "High"—
But, being such a nasty thing,
Adjourned, please, *sine die*.

☞

Cold Comfort

Awaiting trial on murder charge,
And making no defense,

A prisoner at exercise,
(The cold was most intense)—
"You ought to wear an overcoat
A day like this" when told,
Said "Thank you, Sir, but I must get
Accustomed to the cold."

bloody

versicles

153

NOTES

1. *Horatio Bottomley,* Cresset, 1955.
2. *Songs of the Cell,* Southern, 1928.
3. Also published separately in 1927.

Incest

The author of this verse, Molly Tibbs, used to be a social worker in a mental hospital. She writes:

> There are two popular misconceptions about present-day incest; one is that the ignorant and crowded poor "do it like animals"; the other is that the man (if it is a man) is so overflowing with libido that he cannot restrain himself "even" from his own daughter. The truth, however, is more often that the incest arises from an abnormal mental state in the man. The daughter is often a willing partner.

On a Man Convicted of Incest[1]

They brought him straight from the court
And he stood there before us
Puzzled about all the fuss;
He loved his daughter, *tout court,*
Nothing was more natural—
He taught the elemental.
"Single girl should not know man"
—He approved this tribal ban.
    But a father's love was pure and good
    And he loved her as a good man should.

NOTE

1. Incest became a crime in English law with the Punishment of Incest Act 1908, and is the youngest crime represented in this collection. Before 1908, it was only an ecclesiastical offense.

Larceny

including

bank and

train robbery,

burglary,

highway robbery,

pickpocketing,

poaching, and

shoplifting

☞

Ned Kelly's last stand

Ned Kelly

Ned Kelly, "the last of the bushrangers," is probably best
known today as a recurring subject in the work of the Aus-
tralian artist Sidney Nolan. Aided by sympathizers opposed to
authority of any kind, he and his band of bank robbers and
murderers terrorized the states of Victoria and New South
Wales for two years, and it is said that his capture cost
£115,000. In June 1880, the gang was caught in a hotel at
Glenrowan; as usual, they had with them a large number of
local hostages. Ned Kelly was wounded but managed to es-
cape into the bush. After a siege of seven hours and after the
hostages had gotten away, the police set fire to the hotel; the
bodies of Ned Kelly's brother Dan, Steve Hart, and Joe Byrne
were found in the ruins. During the siege Ned Kelly, wearing
armor made of plow moldboards, advanced on the police
from the bush. The armor was struck by twenty-five bullets,
and it took a bullet in the leg to bring him down. He was tried
for the murder of two policemen, and was hanged in Mel-
bourne on 11 November.

There are several Ned Kelly ballads, a good many of them
with an Irish flavor (his father was a Belfast man who had
been transported to Tasmania).

Oh, Paddy dear, and did you hear the news that's going
round?
On the head of bold Ned Kelly they have placed two thou-
sand pounds,
And on Steve Hart, Joe Byrne, and Dan two thousand more
they'd give,
But if the price was doubled, boys, the Kelly Gang would
live.

'Twas December 'seventy-eight when the Kelly Gang came down,
Just after shooting Kennedy, to famed Euroa town;
To rob the bank of all its gold was their idea that day,
Blood horses they were mounted on to make their getaway.

So Kelly marched into the bank, a check all in his hand,
For to have it changed for money of Scott he did demand.
And when that he refused him he, looking at him straight,
Said, "See here, my name's Ned Kelly, and this here man's my mate."

The safe was quickly gutted then, the drawers turned out as well,
The Kellys being quite polite, like any noble swell.
With flimsies, gold and silver coin, the threepennies and all,
Amounting to two thousand pounds, they made a glorious haul.

"Now hand out all your firearms," the robber boldly said,
"And all your ammunition—or a bullet through your head.
Now get your wife and children—come man, now look alive;
All jump into this buggy and we'll take you for a drive."

They took them to a station about three miles away,
And kept them close imprisoned until the following day.
The owner of the station and those in his employ
And a few unwary travellers their company did enjoy.

An Indian hawker fell in too, as everybody knows;
He came in handy to the gang by fitting them with clothes.
Then with their worn-out clothing they made a few bonfires,
And then destroyed the telegraph by cutting down the wires.

They rode into Jerilderie town at twelve o'clock that night,
Aroused the troopers from their beds and gave them an awful fright.
They took them in their night-shirts, ashamed I am to tell,
They covered them with pistols and locked them in a cell.

They next acquainted the womenfolk that they were going to stay
And take possession of the camp until the following day.
They fed their horses in the stalls without the slightest fear,
Then went to rest their weary limbs till daylight did appear.

The next day being Sunday morn, of course they must be good.
They dressed themselves in troopers' clothes, and Ned he chopped some wood.
No one there suspected them; as troopers they did pass;
And Dan, the most religious one, took the sergeant's wife to Mass.

On Monday morning early, still masters of the ground,
They took their horses to the forge and had them shod all round;
Then back they came and mounted, their plans they laid so well,
In company with the troopers they stuck up the Royal Hotel.

They bailed up all the occupants and placed them in a room,
Saying, "Do as we command you, or death will be your doom."
A Chinese cook "No savvy" cried, not knowing what to fear,
But they brought him to his senses with a lift under the ear.

All who now approached the house just shared a similar fate,
In hardly any time at all they numbered twenty-eight.
They shouted freely for all hands, and paid for what they drank,
And two of them remained in charge, and two went to the bank.

The farce was here repeated as I've already told:
They bailed up all the banker's clerks and robbed them of their gold.
The manager could not be found, and Kelly, in great wrath,
Searched high and low, and luckily, he found him in his bath.

bloody

versicles

160

The robbery o'er, they mounted then to make a quick retreat;
They swept away with all their loot by Morgan's ancient beat;
And where they've gone I do not know (if I did I wouldn't
   tell),
So now, until I hear from them, I'll bid you all farewell.

Jesse James

In 1881, the newly elected governor of Missouri offered large rewards (secretly allocated to him by the railway companies) for the apprehension of the James brothers, Frank and Jesse, and members of their gang, who specialized in bank and train robbery, with murder as a side effect. The rewards were devised as an incentive to treachery, and on Monday, 3 April 1882, at a house in St. Joseph, Missouri, where Jesse James was living under the name of Thomas Howard, a member of the gang, Bob Ford, shot him in the back when he was standing on a chair to dust a picture of his favorite horse. Some months later, the consumptive Frank James gave himself up. He was tried on 21 August 1883. The jury, swayed by an eloquent speech in his defense and ignoring the evidence of several eyewitnesses, brought in a verdict of not guilty, and the nattily dressed Frank settled down on his father-in-law's farm and lived to a ripe old age.

Writing in the *Springfield Leader* of 18 October 1933, Robert L. Kennedy recalled:

Soon after the killing of James a ten-foot poem, set to music, came out and was sung on the streets of Springfield quite frequently. It told how Jesse James had a wife and she warned him all her life and the children they were brave and the dirty little coward who shot Mr. Howard and they laid poor Jesse in the grave.[1] It caused tears to be shed; it was the Mark Anthony eulogy at the bier of Caesar. An old blind woman used to stand in front of the court house in Springfield and sing it by the hour; mourners used to drop coins in her tin can. She went up to Richmond, Mo., and was singing her sad

REWARD!

- DEAD OR ALIVE -

$5,000.00/x x will be paid for **the capture** of the men who robbed the bank at

NORTHFIELD, MINN.

They are believed to be **Jesse James and** his Band, or the Youngers.

All officers are warned to use precaution in making arrest.   These are the **most** desperate men in America.

Take no chances! Shoot to kill!!

J. H. McDonald,
SHERIFF

song with tears in her voice when she found herself slapped and kicked into the middle of the street. Bob Ford's sister happened to be passing that way.

Most of the Jesse James ballads are variations on the theme of his betrayal. This one is said to have been composed by a man in Arkansas who often entertained the James brothers in his cabin:

> Jesse James he was a man
> That was knowed through all the land,
> For Jesse he was bold an' bad an' brave,
> But the dirty little coward
> That murdered Mister Howard
> Has went an' laid pore Jesse in his grave.
>
> Hit was on a Friday night,
> An' the moon a-shining bright,
> An' Bob Ford had been hidin' in a cave.
> He had ate of Jesse's bread,
> He had slept in Jesse's bed,
> But he went an' laid pore Jesse in his grave.

NOTE

1. The usually quoted words are:

> Jesse James's lovely wife
> Became a widder all her life,
> Though her children they were brave.
> Oh, the dirty little coward
> That shot poor "Mister Howard"
> And laid Jesse James in the grave!

Bonnie and Clyde

Although the Barrow Gang—led by Clyde Barrow, a diminutive, psychopathic, sexually indeterminate saxophone player, the last person that anyone in *his* right mind would have bought a used getaway car from—achieved little in the way of loot from their raids on small-town banks, petrol stations, greasy-spoon transport cafés, and establishments called Piggly Wiggly stores (their largest haul was $1,500), they were responsible, between them, for at least eighteen murders.

On 23 May 1934, a Wednesday, Barrow and his moll, Bonnie Parker, her nymphomania only whetted by their sharing of beds, rumble seats, and dry ditches in the course of their strange odyssey over the previous four years or so, were killed in an ambush near Arcadia, Louisiana. Clyde, who was twenty-five, and who had been driving with his shoes off, had not had time to put them on; Bonnie, who was twenty-three, had not had time to swallow a mouthful of ham sandwich that she had bitten off a moment before Clyde stamped his tartan-socked foot, probably painfully, on the brake pedal. (Why anyone should have bothered to count the number of bullets fired into the car by the ambushing party, I have no idea, but the total was reported as 167; assuming that the counter was good at sums, and since there is no reason to suppose that the ambushers were better shots than was usually so, it is reasonable to guess that some three hundred bullets were fired with the intention of striking the car or its occupants.)

Bonnie Parker has been described as "crime's answer to Elizabeth Barrett Browning," but, as the following examples of her work show, the comparison is not strictly accurate.

We, each of us, have a good alibi
For being down here in the joint;
But few of them are really justified,
If you get right down to the point.

You have heard of a woman's glory
Being spent on a downright cur.
Still you can't always judge the story
As true being told by her.

As long as I stayed on the island
And heard confidence tales from the gals,
There was only one interesting and truthful,
It was the story of Suicide Sal.

Now Sal was a girl of rare beauty,
Tho' her features were somewhat tough,
She never once faltered from duty,
To play on the up and up.

Sal told me this tale on the evening
Before she was turned out free,
And I'll do my best to relate it
Just as she told it to me.

I was born on a ranch in Wyoming,
Not treated like Helen of Troy,
Was taught that rods were rulers,
And ranked with greasy cowboys.

Further verses were intended, but Bonnie was interrupted
by the arrival of the police outside the house where she and
the rest of the gang were staying. This happened at Joplin,
Missouri, in April 1933. The gang escaped, leaving two po-
licemen dead; a search of the house revealed an arsenal of ri-
fles in an upstairs room and the unfinished poem on the
dining-room table.

Towards the end of July 1933, following the killing of Buck
Barrow, Clyde's elder brother, and the capture of his wife

Blanche (a preacher's daughter who put her fingers in her ears during gunfights), Bonnie composed her masterpiece, "The Story of Bonnie and Clyde," and sent it to a Dallas newspaper to be published after her death:

You've heard the story of Jesse James—
Of how he lived and died.
If you're still in need
Of something to read,
Here's the story of Bonnie and Clyde.

Now Bonnie and Clyde are the Barrow Gang.
I'm sure you all have read
How they rob and steal
And those who squeal
Are usually found dying or dead.

They call them cold-hearted killers;
They say they are heartless and mean;
But I say this with pride,
That I once knew Clyde
When he was honest and upright and clean.

But the laws fooled around,
Kept taking him down
And locking him up in a cell,
Till he said to me,
I'll never be free,
So I'll meet a few of them in hell!

The road was so dimly lighted;
There were no highway signs to guide;
But they made up their minds,
If all roads were blind,
They wouldn't give up till they died.

The road gets dimmer and dimmer;
Sometimes you can hardly see;
But it's fight man to man,
And do all you can,
For they know they can never be free.

If they try to act like citizens,
And rent them a nice little flat,
About the third night
They're invited to fight
By a submachine-gun rat-tat-tat.

They don't think they are too tough or desperate,
They know the law always wins,
They have been shot at before
But they do not ignore
That death is the wages of sin.

From heartbreaks some people have suffered,
From weariness some people have died,
But take it all in all,
Our troubles are small,
Till we get like Bonnie and Clyde.

Some day they will go down together,
And they will bury them side by side.
To a few it means grief,
To the law it's relief,
But it's death to Bonnie and Clyde.

Bonnie and Clyde were not buried side by side. His
colander-like remains were interred next to his brother Buck's
less punctured ones in a cemetery at Dallas, in their home-
state of Texas. Bonnie's laying to rest was in two installments:
her first burial (at which a quartet sang "Beautiful Isle of
Somewhere") was in the Fish Trap Cemetery, not far from
her place of birth, Rowena, also in Texas; her second—orga-
nized, it seems, because someone had tardily decided that
Fish Trap was too unromantic-sounding a place for the end of
the legend that was already being concocted—was in the
Crown Hill Memorial Park. If only as an example of the no-
torious inaccuracy of epitaphs, it is worth quoting the lines in-
scribed on the headstone above one of Bonnie Parker's graves:

As the flowers are all made sweeter
By the sunshine and the dew,

So this old world is made brighter
By the lives of folks like you.[1]

NOTE

1. Equally inappropriate words were inscribed on the gravestone of Belle
Starr (1848–89), the American outlaw known as "the petticoat of the plains"
whose crimes included horse theft, murder, and torture for gain. Her epitaph
is said to have been composed by her illegitimate daughter, Pearl:

> Shed not for her the bitter tear,
> Nor give the heart to vain regret;
> 'Tis but the casket that lies here,
> The gem that fills it sparkles yet.

John Dillinger

The killing of John Dillinger, the only bank robber ever to have a fan club, is part of American folk history.[1] Rumanian-born Anna Sage had excellent reasons for betraying him: as well as the $10,000 reward offered for his capture, she was promised FBI assistance in fighting a deportation order for running a disorderly house. On the swelteringly hot night of Friday, 22 July 1934, Anna Sage, wearing an orange skirt as a "marker," went with Dillinger and Polly Hamilton, the girl Mrs. Sage had "arranged" for him, to see *Manhattan Melody*, starring Clark Gable, at the Biograph cinema in Chicago. The film ended and the three of them strolled out into the street. At a cigar-lighting signal from an agent named Melvin Purvis, the posse of FBI men closed in. Mrs. Sage, her orange skirt turned red by the lights under the marquee, had already dropped back; and Polly Hamilton, seeing men with guns, broke away. As Dillinger ran into an alley, he was hit by four bullets, one at almost point-blank range in the back of the neck. He died at once.[2] Crowds of people struggled to dip their handkerchiefs in his blood, and later that night, thousands streamed past his body while it was lying in state at the mortuary. The next day, someone chalked these lines on the wall of the alley:

> Stranger, stop and wish me well,
> Just say a prayer for my soul in Hell.
> I was a good fellow, most people said,
> Betrayed by a woman all dressed in red.

NOTES

1. For details of the life and crimes of Dillinger, and of other American outlaws of the early thirties (including the Barrow Gang), see *The Dillinger Days* by John Toland, Arthur Barker, 1963.

WANTED

JOHN HERBERT DILLINGER

On June 23, 1934, HOMER S. CUMMINGS, Attorney General of the United States, under the authority vested in him by an Act of Congress approved June 6, 1934, offered a reward of

$10,000.00

for the capture of John Herbert Dillinger or a reward of

$5,000.00

for information leading to the arrest of John Herbert Dillinger.

DESCRIPTION

Age, 32 years; Height, 5 feet 7-1/8 inches; Weight, 153 pounds; Build, medium; Hair, medium chestnut; Eyes, grey; Complexion, medium; Occupation, machinist; Marks and scars, 1/2 inch scar back left hand, scar middle upper lip, brown mole between eyebrows.

All claims to any of the aforesaid rewards and all questions and disputes that may arise as among claimants to the foregoing rewards shall be passed upon by the Attorney General and his decisions shall be final and conclusive. The right is reserved to divide and allocate portions of any of said rewards as between several claimants. No part of the aforesaid rewards shall be paid to any official or employee of the Department of Justice.

If you are in possession of any information concerning the whereabouts of John Herbert Dillinger, communicate immediately by telephone or telegraph collect to the nearest office of the Division of Investigation, United States Department of Justice, the local addresses of which are set forth on the reverse side of this notice.

JOHN EDGAR HOOVER, DIRECTOR,
DIVISION OF INVESTIGATION,
UNITED STATES DEPARTMENT OF JUSTICE,
WASHINGTON, D. C.

June 25, 1934

2. According to a quaint, book-length theory thought up by Jay Robert Nash and Ron Offen (*Dillinger: Dead or Alive?*, Regnery, Chicago, 1970), the man who died in the alley wasn't Dillinger but a man who looked exactly like him.

Charlie Peace

Farewell my dear son, by us all beloved
Thou art gone to dwell in the mansions above
In the bosum of Jesus who sits on the throne
Thou art anxiously waiting for us to come home.

☛

> There is a flower, a gentle flower,
> That blooms in each shaded spot
> And gently to the heart it speaks
> Forget me not.

Those verses were written by Charlie Peace, the first from prison when he heard of the death of his infant son, the second to accompany a birthday present to his daughter. Peace, who was born in Angel Court, Sheffield, on 14 May 1832, was a burglar and a murderer; "he was also a violinist, a reciter of monologues,[1] a sanctimonious humbug, an animal lover, an ardent pacifist, woolweaver, and picture framer."[2] Arrested in a Blackheath garden (but only after he had shot a policeman in the arm), he was tried at Leeds for the murder of a neighbor with whose wife he had been associating. Found guilty, he confessed to an earlier murder. The day before his execution, he prepared his own memorial card:

In Memory of Charles Peace
who was executed in Armley Prison
Tuesday, February 25th, 1879
Aged 47.
For that I don but never intended.

He commented on his last meal: "This is bloody rotten bacon"; and later, when a warder ordered him out of the lavatory, complained: "You're in a hell of a hurry. Who's going to be hanged this morning, you or me?"

David Ward records:[3] "Even now there are echoes of that world of gaslight and squalor in the shrill voices of the children who, playing in the streets, still sing as a chant when skipping rope:

"I love Charlie
Charlie was a thief
Charlie killed a copper
Charlie came to grief
Charlie came to our house
Stole some bread and jam
Eat my mother's pudden
Eat my father's ham
When the coppers caught him
They hung him on a rope
Poor old Charlie
You haven't got a hope."

NOTES

1. See page 204.
2. *Encyclopaedia of Murder*, Colin Wilson and Pat Pitman, Arthur Barker, 1961.
3. *King of the Lags*, Souvenir Press, 1989.

A Young Offender

From an early nineteenth-century broadsheet:

*The Dreadful Life and Confession of a Boy
Aged Twelve Years*

With horror we attempt to relate the progress of evil,
generally prevailing among children, through the cor-
rupt example of wicked parents; though we are con-
strained to confess that many a child, through bad
company, wickedly follow the dictates of their own will,
and often bring the hoary heads of honest parents with
sorrow to the grave. The horrors of a public conscience
crieth to heaven for vengeance against such wretched
parents as belonged to T. King, who after eloping from
their native place, took obscure lodgings in East Smith-
field, where they harbored the vilest creatures, and
wickedly encouraged the only son in lying, stealing, &c.
At the age of seven years the parish humanely bound
him an apprentice but his wickedness soon caused his
master to discharge him. He was afterwards bound to a
chimney sweeper in the borough, who soon repenteth
having taken him, for he plundered every place that he
was sent to work at, for which not only correction but
imprisonment ensued. His master being an honest man,
brought him twice back with some property he had sto-
len, which obtained him pardon and prevented him be-
ing transported.

Lastly, his parents made him desert his master, and
bound him to a gang of thieves who sent him down the
chimney of a jeweller in Swallow Street, where he art-
fully unbolted the shop window, out of which his com-
panions cut a pane of glass, and he handed a
considerable quantity of articles to them; but the noise

he made alarmed the family, and he was taken into cus-
tody, but the others escaped.

He was tried at the last Old Bailey Sessions, found
guilty, and sentenced to die in the twelfth year of his
age. After his sentence the confession he made struck
those around him with horror, stating the particulars of
several murders and robberies. We hope the dreadful
example of this wretched youth may produce a lasting
warning to the world at large.

> Give ear, ye tender mothers dear,
> And when this tale you read
> Of a little boy of twelve years old,
> 'Twill make your hearts to bleed.
> Condemn'd of late for shocking crimes,
> Through his parents' deeds you see;
> You'll weep and cry to see him die
> Upon the gallows tree.
>
> When he was sentenced at the bar,
> The Court was drown'd in tears
> To see a child so soon cut off,
> All in his infant years.
> His mother mad with piercing cries,
> And tearing her hair she went;
> In Bedlam's chains she now remains,
> And his father's to prison sent.
>
> The hardest heart would melt with grief
> To hear this boy's sad moan,
> At the bar he begg'd and pray'd for life
> When his sentence was made known.
> To pick pockets at fair he then declar'd
> His parents made him comply,
> And to join a cruel mob, to murder and rob,
> For which he is forc'd to die.
>
> What must such wretched parents think
> Who train their children so,
> To lead their offspring to the brink
> Of everlasting woe.

Their hearts must be more hard than steel
And deaf to nature's ties,
To plunge their children in such guilt
And hear their piercing cries.

Each heart humane will feel with pain
This poor boy's piteous case,
His shameless parents did him bring
Into this horrid place.
Cropt like a flower before its time,
Which trodden down does lie,
He's doom'd all in his blooming prime,
A shameful death to die.

Be warned, my little children dear,
By this poor boy's downfall,
Keep from dishonest courses clear
And GOD will bless you all.
O, think of this poor little boy,
Lament his woeful state,
Condemn'd to die on a gallows high,
How dreadful is his fate.[1]

NOTE

1. It appears that Master T. King was reprieved from the death sentence.

Burglar's Lament

To the Celebrated Mr. Chubb
of the Patent Locks

I met a cracksman coming down the Strand,
Who said, "A huge cathedral, piled of stone,
Stands in a churchyard near Martin's-le-Grand,
Where keeps St. Paul his sacredotal throne.
A street runs by it on the north-west. There,
For cab and bus, is writ 'No Thoroughfare':
The mayor and councilmen do so command;
And in that street a shop, with many a box,
Upon whose sign these fateful words I scanned:—
'My name is Chubb, that makes the Patent Locks;
Look on my work, ye burglars, and despair.'
Here I did pause, like one who sees a blight
Crush all his hopes, and sighed, with drooping air,
'Our game is up, my covey, blow me tight!' "

JACK FIREBLOOD,
Flowers of Hemp, 1841

Stone Stealers

The theft by four Scottish students of the Stone of Destiny (or Stone of Scone) from Westminster Abbey on Christmas night, 1950, inspired many songs. This is one of them:

Noo Sherlock Holmes
(Tune: Barbara Allen)

O, Sherlock Holmes is deid lang syne
In some forgotten garret,
But aa o' youse hae heard the news
O Sup'rintendent Barratt.

He cam' up here in Janiveer,
The day it was a Monday;
He crossed the border deep in snaw
And wished ti Hell he hadnae!

For aa he got whin he cam' North
Wis "Here!" an' "There!" an' "Yonder!"
He fleed aboot in a high-speed caur,
But his clues wad only daunder.

"Four days o' frosts, ah want nae mair,"
He tellt the Scottish polis,
"Ye kin keep your Stane, an' the yins thit taen't!"
And aff he gaed hame, clueless.

O, Sherlock Holmes is deid lang syne
In some forgotten garret,
But that's guid luck, for Holmes wad boke
To hear the name o' Barratt.

Over a year after the theft, the stone was found in Arbroath Abbey.

In June 1969, another attempt was made to steal the stone from the Coronation chair in Westminster Abbey. "Pendennis" of *The Observer* reported:

Abbey officials discovered broken glass and half-sawn bars in a window of the Islop Chapel. The police had already received a tip-off that a theft would take place. The would-be thieves clearly wanted to break into the Abbey via the Islop Chapel, 100 yards away from the Stone. The general feeling is that any Nationalist commando unable to even get past old-fashioned bars would have been completely foxed by the modern alarm system which guards the Stone itself.

We believe the thieves were four young Scotsmen—*not* members of the Scottish Liberation Army. Their motive might have been an attempt to upstage the Welsh Nationalists and the investiture [of Prince Charles at Caernarvon]. The Stone has always been a target for Scottish extremists who've never forgiven the original theft from Scone Abbey in 1296 by Edward I. . . . But last week's attempted theft wasn't just an amateur job: it didn't even get any publicity. Which leaves a more plausible motive: the Scotsmen were confidence tricksters.

Several months ago, a number of people in and around the Nationalist movement in Scotland were approached by the thieves and shown a portfolio of blown-up photographs of the Stone in its setting beneath the Coronation chair. . . . They also explained that one of their gang was a qualified engineer, well able to take care of the Abbey's alarm system. The gang then went on to explain that, for a successful robbery, they would need funds for special equipment, airline tickets, and getaway cars.

One attempt was made to get the money from a newspaper—to the extent of £400—in return for an exclusive story. They didn't succeed. We believe that the young men subsequently found at least one backer in a Scottish businessman. Having raised the money, the gang then completed the operation by making a token attempt, explaining their failure, it is said, by blaming the unexpected arrival of dawn over Westminster.

Dick Turpin

I think "Dick Turpin" was the first criminal name I ever
heard. As a very small boy, walking—but only just—with my
parents on Wimbledon Common, I was told that some hoof-
marks in the gravel had been made by Turpin on his ride to
York. I know now that the ride to York is simply part of the
legend, and that Black Bess was sired by the mythmakers;
even so, whenever I am on the common I still have to think
twice about any hoof-marks I see.

Born in 1706, Turpin was executed at York on 7 April
1739, after hiring five mourners for his funeral.

My Poor Black Bess

When fortune, blind goddess, she fled my abode,
Old friends proved ungrateful, I took to the road;
To plunder the wealthy to aid my distress,
I bought thee to aid me, my poor Black Bess.

When dark sable night its mantle had thrown
O'er the bright face of nature, how oft we have gone
To famed Hounslow Heath, though an unwelcome guest
To the minions of fortune, my poor Black Bess.

How silent thou stood when a carriage I've stopped,
And their gold and their jewels its inmates I've dropped;
No poor man I plundered or e'er did oppress
The widow or orphan, my poor Black Bess.

When Argus-eyed justice did me hotly pursue,
From London to York like lightning we flew;
No toll-bar could stop thee, thou the river didst breast,
And in twelve hours reached it, my poor Black Bess.

But fate darkens o'er us, despair is my lot,
The law does pursue us, through a cock which I shot;
To save me, poor brute, thou didst do thy best,
Thou art worn out and weary, my poor Black Bess.

Hark the bloodhounds approach, they never shall have
A beast like thee, noble, so faithful and brave;
Thou must die, my dumb friend, though it does me distress,
There, there, I have shot thee, my poor Black Bess.

And in after ages, when I'm dead and gone,
This tale will be handed from father to son,
My fate some may pity, but all will confess,
'Twas in kindness I killed thee, my poor Black Bess.

No one can say that ingratitude dwelt
In the bosum of Turpin, 'twas a vice he ne'er felt;
I shall die like a man, and soon be at rest,
Then farewell for ever, my poor Black Bess.

ANON

Dick Turpin, a drawing by "Phiz"

To the Hero of Rookwood

Turpin! thou shouldst be living at this hour!
England hath need of thee: common and fen,
Hounslow and Bagshot, tavern, boozing-ken,
The triple tree, and stone jug's lonely bower,
Have forfeited their ancient English dower
Of dashing Tobygloaks.[1] We are sneaks, not men.
Oh! raise us up, return to us again.
And give us will to take a purse and power!
Thy soul from vulgar filchers dwelt apart:
Thou hadst a steed, whose hoofs devoured the lea;
Under the midnight heavens, majestic, free,
Thou tookst the air on the King's common way,
Whistling serenely, and, with regal air,
The lieges under tribute oft didst lay.

JACK FIREBLOOD,
Flowers of Hemp, 1841

NOTE

1. Highwaymen.

Claude Duval

A living sea of eager human faces,
  A thousand bosums, throbbing all as one,
Walls, windows, balconies, all sorts of places,
  Holding their crowds of gazers to the sun:
  Through the hushed groups low-buzzing murmurs run;
And on the air, with slow reluctant swell,
Comes the dull funeral-boom of old Sepulcher's bell.

Oh, joy in London now! In festal measure
  Be spent the evening of this festive day!
For thee is opening now a high-strung pleasure;
  Now, even now, in yonder press-yard, they
  Strike from his limbs and fetters loose away!
A little while, and he, the brave Duval,
Will issue forth, serene, to glad and greet you all.

"Why comes he not? Say, wherefore doth he tarry?"
  Starts the inquiry loud from every tongue.
"Surely," they cry, "that tedious Ordinary
  His tedious psalms must long ere this have sung—
  Tedious to him that's waiting to be hung!"
But hark! old Newgate's doors fly wide apart.
"He comes, he comes!" A thrill shoots through each
  gazer's heart.

Joined in the stunning cry ten thousand voices,
  All Smithfield answered to the loud acclaim.
"He comes, he comes!" and every breast rejoices,
  As down Snow Hill the shout tumultuous came,
  Bearing to Holborn's crowd the welcome fame.

"He comes, he comes!" and each holds back his breath—
Some ribs are broke, and some few scores are crushed to
 death.

With step majestic to the cart advances
 The dauntless Claude, and springs into his seat,
He feels that on him now are fixed the glances
 Of many a Briton bold and maiden sweet,
 Whose hearts responsive to his glories beat.
In him the honor of "The Road" is centered,
And all the hero's fire into his bosum entered.

His was the transport—his the exultation
 Of Rome's great generals, when, from afar,
Up to the Capitol, in the Ovation,
 They bore with them, in the triumphal car,
 Rich gold and gems, the spoils of foreign war
Io Triumphe! They forgot their clay.
E'en so Duval, who rode in glory on his way.

His laced cravat, his kids of purest yellow,
 The many-tinted nosegay in his hand,
His large black eyes, so fiery, yet so mellow,
 Like the old vintages of Spanish land,
 Locks clustering o'er a brow of high command,
Subdue all hearts: and as, up Holborn's steep,
Toils the slow car of death, e'en cruel butchers weep.

He saw it, but he heeded not. His story,
 He knew, was graven on the page of Time.
Tyburn to him was as a field of glory,
 Where he must stoop to death his head sublime,
 Hymned in full many an elegiac rhyme.
He left his deeds behind him, and his name—
For he, like Caesar, had lived long enough for fame.

He quailed not, save when, as he raised the chalice—
 St. Giles's bowl—filled with the mildest ale,
To pledge the crowd, on her—his beauteous Alice—
 His eyes alighted, and his cheek grew pale.
 She, whose sweet breath was like the spicy gale,

She whom he fondly deemed his own dear girl,
Stood with a tall dragoon, drinking long draughts of purl.

He bit his lip—it quivered but a moment—
   Then passed his hand across his flushing brows;
He could have spared so forcible a comment
   Upon the constancy of woman's vows.
   One short sharp pang his hero-soul allows;
But in the bowl he drowned the stinging pain,
And on his pilgrimage went calmly forth again.

A princely group of England's noblest daughters
   Stood on a balcony, suffused with grief,
Diffusing fragrance round them, of strong waters,
   And waving many a snowy handkerchief;
   Then glowed the prince of highwaymen and thief!
His soul was touched with a seraphic gleam—
That woman could be false was but a mocking dream.

And now, his bright career of triumph ended,
   His chariot stood beneath the triple tree.
The law's grim finisher to its boughs ascended,
   And fixed the hempen bandages, while he
   Bowed to the throng, then bade the cart go free.
The cart rolled on, and left him dangling there,
Like famed Mohammed's tomb, uphung midway in air.

As droops the cup of the surcharged lily,
   Beneath the surly buffets of the storm
Or the soft petals of the daffodilly,
   When Sirius is uncomfortably warm,
   So dropped his head upon his manly form,
While floated in the breeze his tresses brown.
He hung the stated time, and then they cut him down.

With soft and tender care the trainbands bore him,
   Just as they found him, nightcap, rope, and all,
And placed this neat, though plain, inscription o'er him,
   Among the anatomies in Surgeons' Hall,[2]
   THESE ARE THE BONES OF THE RENOWNED DUVAL!

There still they tell us, from their glassy case,
He was the last, the best, of all that noble race.

BON GAULTIER, 1841

NOTES

1. Claude Duval, French-born highwayman, who is said to have danced a coranto with a woman on Hounslow Heath before robbing her husband of £100. Nothing like as chivalrous as the legend makes out, he was arrested while in a drunken stupor and executed on 21 January 1670, when he was twenty-six years of age.

2. Not so. After lying in state in the Tangier Tavern at St. Giles, he was buried in the center aisle of St. Paul's Church, Covent Garden (now known as "the actors' church"), beneath a stone bearing this epitaph:

> Here lies Du Vall: Reader, if male thou art,
> Look to thy purse; if female, to thy Heart . . .
> Old Tyburn's glory, England's illustrious thief,
> Du Vall, the ladies' Joy, Du Vall the ladies' grief.

The Pickpocket

Miss Dolly Trull

Of all the mots in this here jug,
There's none like saucy Dolly;
And but to view her dimber mug
Is e'er excuse for folly.
She runs such precious cranky rigs
With pinching wedge and lockets,
Yet she's the toast of all the prigs
Through stealing hearts and pockets.

Just twig Miss Dolly at a hop—
She tries to come the graces!
To gain her end she will not stop
And all the swells she chases.
She ogles, nods, and patters flash
To ev'ry flatty cully
Until she frisks him, at a splash
Of rhino, wedge, and tully.

PIERCE EGAN,
Captain Macheath, 1842

Mot = girl or woman; dimber mug = pretty face; cranky rig = criminal
trick; wedge = silver; prig = pickpocket; patters flash = talks in the lan-
guage of the underworld; flatty cully = simpleton; frisk = search pockets;
rhino = money. Tully, it seems, was invented by Egan when he could not
think of a rhyme for cully.

The Poacher

A Serious Ballad

"But a bold pheasantry, their country's pride,
When once destroyed can never be supplied."
GOLDSMITH

Bill Blossom was a nice young man,
    And drove the Bury coach;
But bad companions were his bane,
    And egg'd him on to poach.

They taught him how to net the birds,
    And how to noose the hare;
And with a wiry terrier,
    He often set a snare.

Each "shiny night" the moon was bright,
    To park, preserve, and wood
He went, and kept the game alive,
    By killing all he could.

Land-owners, who had rabbits, swore
    That he had this demerit—
Give him an inch of warren, he
    Would take a yard of ferret.

At partridges he was not nice;
    And many, large and small,
Without Hall's powder, without lead,
    Were sent to Leaden-Hall.

He did not fear to take a deer
    From forest, park, or lawn;

And without courting lord or duke,
   Used frequently to *fawn*.

Folks who had hares discovered snares—
   His course they could not stop:
No barber he, and yet he made
   Their hares a perfect crop.

To pheasant he was such a foe,
   He tried the keepers' nerves;
They swore he never seem'd to have
   Jam satis of *preserves*.

The Shooter went to beat, and found
   No sporting worth a pin,
Unless he tried the *covers* made
   Of silver, plate, or tin.

In Kent the game was little worth,
   In Surrey not a button;
The Speaker said he often tried
   The *Manors* about *Sutton*.

No county from his tricks was safe;
   In each he tried his lucks,
And when the keepers were in *Beds*,
   He often was at *Bucks*.

And when he went to *Bucks*, alas!
   They always came to *Herts;*
And even *Oxon* used to wish
   That he had his desserts.

But going to his usual *Hants*,
   Old *Cheshire* laid his plots:
He got entrapp'd by legal *Berks*,
   And lost his life in *Notts*.

THOMAS HOOD

The Shoplifter

Oh, don't we live in curious times,
You scarce could be believing,
When Frenchmen fight and Emperors die,
And ladies go a-thieving.

A beauty of the West-end went,
Around a shop she lingers,
And there upon some handkerchiefs
She clapped her pretty fingers.
Into the shop she gently popped,
The world is quite deceiving
When ladies have a notion got
To ramble out a-thieving.

Thieving is a naughty trade
As I unto you will state;
If a poor man stole a penny loaf
They'd send him off to Newgate.
They would cause him six months in jail
'Cause in roguery he was dealing,
But here's a lady in a veil
Who rambles out a-stealing.

Her husband when he heard the news
Received a regular twister,
He vowed he'd bleed and jalp her
And her pretty fingers blister,
Because she did not steal for want
Nor was she getting thinner,

She had things to wear and all things nice

And did not want a dinner.

Not very far from Baker Street
This lady in her rigging
Went out so grand, you understand,
To have a turn at prigging,
But lack-a-daisy she got caught,
The shopman he did mark her,
I say, says he, marm, if you please,
Pray what have you been arter?

You have been prigging, marm, says he,
Your looks are quite deceiving,
So help my bob you'll go to quad,
For going out a-thieving.
I would not believe that you could thieve,
You've done it, marm, so clever,
But you are caught as quick as thought,
Oh dear, did you ever.

The draper bawled beneath her shawl,
What do you mean by this, then?
And quickly she was in the hands
Of a stunning great policeman,
Who walked her off, so help my bob,
She really was deceiving,
And the magistrates sent her to quad
For going out a-thieving.

Now ladies all take my advice
And you will always find it,
Honesty is the best policy,
Pray ladies try to mind it,
Don't covet other people's goods
Or be the least deceiving,
Do what is right, lead an honest life,
And don't go out a-thieving

Perjury

Prostitution

Rape, etc.

Treason

Poetic Justice

A Medico-Legal Expert

Perjury

There is a man in London town has made a great sensation,
He swears that he's a baronet, the biggest in the nation.
He went abroad when he was young like Jack to seek his fortune,
And now, returned, he claims to be the Right Sir Roger Tichborne.

There is adequate evidence of the public interest aroused by the Tichborne case, but if further proof be needed, it may be found in the number of verses that the case inspired.

In 1854, Roger Tichborne, "a slight, dark, pale young man, with a soft melancholy eye" who was heir to the Tichborne baronetcy and fortune, sailed from Rio de Janeiro in the ship *La Bella,* which was never seen again. Eleven years later, the rather dotty Dowager Lady Tichborne, who had never given up hope that her son was still alive, engaged an Australian agency to circulate a notice offering "a handsome reward" for information about his whereabouts; Thomas Castro, a fat butcher and bankrupt living in Wagga Wagga, New South Wales, came forward with the claim that he was the long-lost heir. He travelled to England, where many friends, associates, and servants of the Tichborne family said that they recognized him as Roger, and then went on to Paris, where the dowager identified him as her son.

> Now they thought Sir Roger he was dead,
> In the Bella he got drowned,
> He travelled Australia over,
> None thought him above ground.
>
> They say the chap that went abroad
> Was naught but skin and bone,

ENCE not DEFIANCE

.. JAMES' GREAT HALL,
REGENT STREET AND PICCADILLY.

WEDNESDAY & THURSDAY EVENINGS,
DECEMBER 11th and 12th.
THE WEEK OF THE CATTLE SHOW.
TWO DEMONSTRATIONS ONLY, commencing at Eight o'clock.

SIR ROGER C. D.

TICHBORNE

Guildford Onslow, Esq., M.P. for Guildford,
G. H. Whalley, Esq., M.P. for Peterborough,
And G. B. SKIPWORTH, Esq.,
Will each be present to support the Claimant, and deliver ADDRESSES on the World-famous

TICHBORNE CASE !
FOR THE BENEFIT OF THE DEFENCE FUND.

Sofa Stalls (numbered), 3s. - Balcony, 2s. - Admission, 1s.
Tickets and Places may be now secured at Mr. Austin's Office, St. James' Hall. Doors open at 7 o'clock.

But the present claimant's far from that,
He weighs six and twenty stone.[1]

They say Lady Tichborne swore to him
By this thing and by that;
She really ought to know him
In spite of all his fat.

The civil case, in which the claimant contested his rights to
the baronetcy, estates, and fortune, began in May 1871 and
dragged on until March of the following year. The evidence,
mainly concerned with the claimant's ability to remember
facts about Roger Tichborne's past, was a Carrollesque con-
coction of disparate ingredients ranging from Euclid's *Pons
Asinorum* (which the claimant thought was a bridge near Rog-
er's school) to a discussion about ears (Roger's were lobeless,
the claimant's were not), and from a story by the claimant that
he—that is, Roger—had slept with his cousin, and that she
had told him she was expecting a baby, to testimony about
Roger's tattoo marks.

About those marks upon him
They've made a great to do.
They say that he's tattoo'd upon
His hoop de dooden doo!

The claim was rejected by the jury, and Castro/Tichborne
was lodged in Newgate to await trial for perjury.

Come now and listen unto me,
Some curious news I bring,
It's about Sir Roger
That I am going to sing;
For one hundred days in Westminster Hall
He boldly stood his ground,
And now of perjury he's accused,
And in Newgate now he's found.

They call him Wagga Wagga,
Which isn't quite a treat,

They say he's fed in Newgate
Upon Australian meat.
The hammock they provided him,
It could not hold his fat,
So they bought him a special bedstead,
Now what do you say to that.

Now if he is an imposter,
He's clever, I am sure,
There was seventeen against him,
Eighty-five to him they swore.
Now if the public had their will,
They would all agree with me,
They would give the claimant the estates,
Then settled the case would be.

As Michael Gilbert says,[2] "The aspect of a poor man pitted against the juggernaut of government produced some slashing versification":

Government finds the money
The Tichborne case to end,
It does not trouble them a bit,
However much they spend.
They're drawing their expenses
From taxes, I'll be bound,
So working men will have to pay
To crush poor Roger down.

The period between the two trials produced a rich crop of verses, including several "Tichborne Alphabets," one of which began,

A stands for Attorney-General, who had so much to say,
He was matched against Sir Roger for fifty pounds a day,

and ended,

Z stands for Zanies, in a jury box a-snoozing,
They let the judge have all his way, now isn't it amusing.

Although most of the publications supported the claimant, there were a few lampoons from the opposition, and someone went to the trouble of composing an anagram (not quite an exact fit):

> Sir Roger Charles Doughty Tichborne, Baronet
> You horrid butcher, Orton;[3] biggest rascal here

The trial for perjury opened in April 1873, with a jury composed of the following:

> *Docwra* and *Paige* the hosiers; *Edwards* milkman
> *Dickins* the linendraper, cook, and silkman
> *Taylor* kamptulicon—and *Turner* shoemaker
> (Of conscientious verdicts each the true maker)
> *Parsons* the lodging house skilled to superintend
> *Sheppard* of Bouverie the faithful friend
> *Winter* the publican who keeps the White Hart

Yᵉ SPECIAL IURYMAN'S DREAM ATTE HYS COMFORTABLE HOSTEL

Richardson ditto; says he sleeps with light heart
Franklin the butcher; *Dunsby*, barber, heyday
For ever with the Lord and with the Lady
God save the Queen! This is the Tichborne Jury
£315 a piece their value, I assure ye.[4]

As the trial dragged on, the members of the jury became
more and more selective in their choice of evidence to digest,
and whiled away much of the time by playing games of the
noughts-and-crosses variety, composing anagrams and acros-
tics, and inventing jokes and riddles. ("Why are all the Tich-
borne jurors Liberal?" asked William Taylor, and gave the
answer, "Because they would vote for an early redistribution
of seats." John Sheppard suggested that the answer to "Why is
the lord chief justice like the Dutchman's little dog?" was "Be-
cause his tail's [tale's] too long.") They also composed many
verses. The following "tandem" verses are thought to be the
work of Taylor:

YE PICTURE of Yᵉ DREAM of Yᵉ JURYMAN'S WIFE

He

What form is this which meets my sight,
And fills my soul with horrid fright
Whene'er I close my eyes at night?
                          The Claimant!

What can this apparition be,
This bulky form I always see,
What may this rotund body be?
                          The Claimant!

What's this that cuts me like a knife,
This sight I see? Why bless my life,
The fellow's flirting with my wife.
                          The Claimant!

Oh! I am sure I shall not rue
The time when they shall give a few
Odd years upon the treadmill to
                          The Claimant!

She

Oh! dark and cold is the cell
In which my loved one is immured,
And I'm sure I think it is well
He was careful his life was insured.

Most unfortunate man of your kin,
Oh! Juryman (special) ill starred,
The gruel you'll find very thin
And the "toke"[5] uncommonly hard.

What a shame you are hurried away
To leave a poor wife all forlorn,
Who'll be weeping for many a day,
And all for the fault of Tichborne.

But my darling, I have an idea
Which my fancy very much tickles,
To Newgate I'll come without fear
And bring you some biscuits and pickles.

The claimant was defended by Dr. Edward Kenealy, a pug-
nacious and loquacious product of the Irish Bar. Trying to
bolster the theory that his client's poor memory for events in
Roger's life was the result of an unhappy youth, Kenealy
made a sustained attack on the Tichborne family. Not content
with that, he also attacked the judges and the prosecution.

Lord Exmouth, who was in court when Kenealy was quot-
ing at length from the writings of "the lewd" de Kock, one of
Roger's favorite authors, composed the following:

Said Kenealy, from drinking and smoking and snuff
    Morality suffers a shock;
But to build up a "Roger" they are not enough.
    You must call in the aid of De Kock.

Seduction made easy, and vice harmless sport
    Are his maxims our morals to shock.
Then t'were best, said the Chief, to keep ladies from Court
    While you are translating De Kock.

So next day an order was posted which ran,
    "No ladies before twelve o'clock."
And Kenealy appeared, and straightway began
    To translate from the works of De Kock.

"I could listen all day," said the Chief with delight,
    Said Mellor, "I don't care a rush
If De Kock should take up both a day and a night."
    "Oh, it's capital really," cried Lush.[6]

Kenealy's rantings and ravings were in vain. On 28 Febru-
ary 1874, the 188th day of the trial, the jury found the claim-
ant guilty, and he was sentenced to fourteen years' penal
servitude. Kenealy's conduct led to his being disbarred by the
Benchers of Gray's Inn.

Fair Play for Tichborne and Kenealy

Give me the man of honest heart,
I like no two-faced dodger,

But one who nobly speaks his part
Like Kenealy did for Roger;
One honest lawyer's found at last
Who'll ne'er desert his client,
He knows right well the cause is just,
He stands up like a giant.

Now when the big-wigs found that he
To them would not be suing,
They knocked their wigs together, boys,
And swore they'd be his ruin;
We dare not do it publicly
For fear t'would cause a riot,
So we'll get the Gray's Inn Benchers
To do it on the quiet.

Sir Roger bears up like a man,
His spirits never lacking,
When he gets out there is no doubt
He'll give his foes a whacking;
His mother worried to her grave,
Her son they'd like to settle,
But Roger shows the world he's made
Of good old English metal.

The claimant earned full remission and was released from
prison after ten years. He died in poverty in 1898.

NOTES

1. No exaggeration.
2. *The Claimant*, Constable, 1957.
3. There was a strong belief that the claimant had started life as Arthur
Orton of Wapping.
4. A reference to the property qualification of a special juryman.
5. Bread.
6. The lord chief justice, Sir Alexander Cockburn, presided at the trial,
assisted by Mr. Justice Mellor and Mr. Justice Lush.

Prostitution / 1

Thomas Hood's "The Bridge of Sighs" was a favorite poem of both Charlie Peace (see page 172) and Henry Wainwright (hanged in 1875 for the murder of his mistress, Harriet Lane); they often recited it as their contribution to musical evenings. During Jack the Ripper's reign of terror, the first stanza became a hackneyed quotation—a ready-made epitaph for the doubly unfortunate victims.

The Bridge of Sighs

"Drown'd! drown'd!"—HAMLET

One more Unfortunate,
Weary of breath,
Rashly importunate,
Gone to her death!

Take her up tenderly,
Lift her with care;
Fashion'd so slenderly,
Young, and so fair!

Look at her garments
Clinging like cerements;
Whilst the wave constantly
Drips from her clothing;
Take her up instantly,
Loving, not loathing.—

Touch her not scornfully;
Think of her mournfully,
Gently and humanly;

Not of the stains of her,
All that remains of her
Now is pure womanly.

Make no deep scrutiny
Into her mutiny
Rash and undutiful:
Past all dishonor
Death has left on her
Only the beautiful.

Still, for all slips of hers,
One of Eve's family—
Wipe those poor lips of hers
Oozing so clammily.

Loop up her tresses
Escaped from the comb,
Her fair auburn tresses;
Whilst wonderment guesses
Where was her home?

Who was her father?
Who was her mother?
Had she a sister?
Had she a brother?
Or was there a dearer one
Still, and a nearer one
Yet, than all other?

Alas! for the rarity
Of Christian charity
Under the sun!
Oh! it was pitiful!
Near a whole city full,
Home she had none!

Sisterly, brotherly,
Fatherly, motherly,
Feelings had changed;
Love, by harsh evidence,

Thrown from its eminence;
Even God's providence
Seeming estranged.

Where the lamps quiver
So far in the river,
With many a light
From window and casement,
From garret to basement,
She stood, with amazement,
Houseless by night.

The bleak wind of March
Made her tremble and shiver;
But not the dark arch,
Or the black flowing river:
Mad from life's history,
Glad to death's mystery,
Swift to be hurl'd—
Anywhere, anywhere,
Out of the world!

In she plunged boldly,
No matter how coldly
The rough river ran,—
Over the brink of it,
Picture it—think of it,
Dissolute man!
Lave in it, drink of it,
Then, if you can!

Take her up tenderly,
Lift her with care;
Fashion'd so slenderly,
Young, and so fair!

Ere her lips frigidly
Stiffen too rigidly,
Decently,—kindly,—
Smoothe and compose them:

And her eyes, close them,
Staring so blindly!

Dreadfully staring
Thro' muddy impurity,
As when with the daring
Last look of despairing,
Fix'd on futurity.

Perishing gloomily,
Spurr'd by contumely,
Cold inhumanity,
Burning insanity,
Into her rest,—
Cross her hands humbly,
As if praying dumbly,
Over her breast!

Owning her weakness,
Her evil behavior,
And leaving, with meekness,
Her sins to her Savior!

Prostitution / 2

On 12 June 1969, *The Stiffkey Scandals of 1932*, devised by David Wright, with score by David Wood, opened at the Queen's Theatre, London. It told the story of the ecclesiastical trial of the Reverend Harold Davidson for immoral conduct and its extraordinary aftermath. In a program note, David Wright outlined the events that led to the trial:

> Davidson found Stiffkey [on the north coast of Norfolk] a small parish, and his parishioners few. A man of unbounded energy, he found little in the village to engage his evangelical zeal, and he soon started to spend much of his time in London in rescue and welfare work. His parishioners rarely saw him except on Sundays, but in London he became an increasingly familiar figure as he labored unceasingly to protect young and lonely girls from the snares and pitfalls that he saw menacing them from every side. Girls who had, unfortunately, already "fallen" he attempted to set once again on the right road. None doubted Davidson's dedication to this missionary work, but some were confused as to his motives. Among these, unfortunately, was the Bishop of Norwich, whose increasing doubts led him, in 1931, to hire a firm of private investigators, the Arrows Detective Agency, to inquire into the exact nature of the Reverend Davidson's work in London.

One of David Wood's songs was an account of a typical day in the life of the Reverend Davidson, as seen through the eyes of one of the private detectives:

The Lament of Inglebert Ralph Thole

I've had embezzlements, adulteries,
Shopliftings by the score—

A postcard dating from the Blackpool period of the rector's life, when he was a regular feature among the sideshows of the Golden Mile. It was no doubt offered for sale by the rector in an attempt to raise additional funds to clear his name.

But I've never had a case like this before.
A typical day
Spent the Davidson way
Is scarcely what you'd call a bore.

Seven A.M.,
Left his digs,
Went to Waterloo,
Met Mavis Briggs;
At seven forty-four
Knocked upon the door
Of Edith Tate—
Left at half-past eight—
Had a bacon and egg
With Amelia Clegg
In a restaurant that's in the Strand,
And at nine thirty-one precisely
He shook her hand.

Ten twenty-two,
Leicester Square,
Met Irene James
And touched her hair;
Eleven thirty-three,
Had a cup of tea
With Evelyn Boon—
Said goodbye at noon—
Took a taxi to go
To a cafe in So-
-ho, and met a prostitute called Pat,
And at twelve forty-three precisely
Took off her hat.

At one o five it started to rain;
By now the case was proving
A bit of a strain.

One fifty-eight,
Finished meal,
Went to matinee
with Dora Steel;

At twenty-five past four
Waited at stage door
For Phyllis Dee—
Went to Lyon's for tea—
Took her back to her flat,
Then came back and met Pat
In a public house and bought a drink;
And at six twenty-one precisely
Gave her a wink.

Seven P.M.,
Off he sped,
Missed an omnibus
So walked instead;
At seven forty-eight
Met a girl whose date
Had not turned up—
Took her out to sup—
And then asked her to go
To a cinema show
Where the film was sad and made them weep,
And at nine twenty-three precisely
I fell asleep.

Davidson, whose clerical title was Rector of Stiffkey, was known to many of his parishioners as "little Jim"; to the Nippies in the London teashops which he frequented with his girls, he was "the mormon"; but he himself preferred to be called "the Prostitutes' Padre":

I'm called the Prostitutes' Padre;
It's the proudest title
That a priest could hold;
I know I'm doing right,
Ever fighting the good fight,
Trying to bring new lambs into the fold.

I am the Prostitutes' Padre,
And I see no reason
Why my work is wrong;

By criticizing me
You're just saying, "Leave them be,
Leave them on the streets where they belong."

My purpose is to save,
Not just to buy a girl her dinner—
But that's a paltry price to pay
For one repentant sinner.

I am the Prostitutes' Padre,
And it's true I help the
Lowest of the low;
To you they don't seem much,
Girls that you would never touch—
I can wash them white as driven snow.

You can't say it's their fault
That they have come to this position;
They need someone to give them hope,
And that has been my mission.

I am the Prostitutes' Padre
And I'll keep crusading
Till the day I die;
The Church should get about,
Help these girls, not cast them out—
Jesus thought them worth it; so do I.

I believe with all my soul,
Although to you it may sound silly,
That if our Lord were born again
He'd work in Piccadilly.

I'm proud to be their guide,
Knowing Christ is by my side,
And each day
I'll fervently pray
That he'll help me be
The Prostitutes' Padre.

The reports from the detective agency, jam-packed with-
data but containing precious little evidence of immoral

conduct, caused the Bishop of Norwich to become increasingly agitated; it seems unlikely, however, that he would have brought the action against Davidson had it not been for a series of articles that appeared in the *Sunday Empire News*.

In June 1932, Davidson was found guilty by the Consistory Court, and in October was unfrocked at a ceremony in Norwich Cathedral. During the next five years Davidson (an ex-actor as well as being an ex-rector) used showmen's gimmicks to publicize his cause and to raise money to clear his name.

The Fight Goes on

If you think
That you can crush me when
You take away my priesthood,
You'll have to think again.

I may have been rejected,
Spurned and spat upon;
The Church has cast me out,
But still the fight goes on.

I cannot wear the cassock
Or the collar any more,
But that won't make me give up
My mission, that's for sure;
I'll take up arms, I'll wage a war,
I'll march for the Lord and fight
All those who stop me working
For what I know is right.

I may have been rejected,
Spurned and spat upon;
The Church has cast me out,
But still the fight goes on.

I may have got no money
Since they took my job away,
But once I was an actor
And now I'll make it pay;
I'll sit in barrels, squat on poles,
My future now is clear:

I'll be a public sideshow,
I'll preach on Blackpool Pier.

I may have been rejected,
Spurned and spat upon;
The Church has cast me out,
But still the fight goes on.

I'll be an entertainer
Then, until I know I've won;
It's worth it to continue
The work I have begun;
I'll suffer scorn, indignity,
The insults the public hurls,
It's worth the degradation
To get back to my girls.

I'm still the Prostitutes' Padre,
But the Church is more cor-
rupt than any whore.
They've turned down my appeal,
It's a wound no one can heal,
I reject them till they change the law.
It's wrong and quite unjust
That I have come to this position,
No other priest must suffer thus,
And that will be my mission.

I may have been rejected,
Spurned and spat upon;
The Church has cast me out,
But still the fight goes on.

Harold Davidson's end was ridiculously appropriate. In the summer of 1937 he signed a contract to lecture in a lion's cage at Skegness Amusement Park. He arrived at the cage to find that there was not one lion but two, a male and a female. Questioning this, he was assured of his safety. He slipped between the bars and, watched by an audience of vacationers, was killed by the male lion, whose name was Freddie.

David Wright says that "the only memorial to his tumultuous Rectorship is his simple but carefully tended grave in the village churchyard at Stiffkey. When I visited it earlier this year daffodils planted by some well-wisher grew beneath a plain marble cross bearing the inscription,

"For on faith in man and genuine love of man
all searching after truth must be founded."

Rape, etc.

I must be careful what I say—or rather, how I say it. An American friend has just sent me a newspaper clipping about the trial of a man, surnamed Calhoun, who is charged with having robbed and raped a young woman, who must have both unnaturally sharp teeth and a tenacious nature, for, either during or immediately after the alleged latter offense, she bit his testicles off. The prosecution and the defense agree that, within half an hour of the separation, Calhoun turned up at a hospital, rather gingerly carrying the detached parts on or in domestic ware of some kind that he had found in the woman's apartment; I cannot make out whether or not the robbery charge relates to the domestic ware, which Calhoun seems to have used as a receptacle, perhaps in the absence of a ten-pin bowler's bag, without the owner's consent. A hospital doctor informed him that the detached parts could not be reattached. If there are exhibits at the trial, no doubt the parts, bottled like Victoria plums, are among them.

In a letter thanking my American friend for the clipping, I wrote this limerick:

> An alleg-ed young rapist, Calhoun,
> Considered his balls quite a boon;
> When they were dismembered,
> He quickly remembered
> To hold them aloft on a spoon.

Treason

Chidiock Tichborne[1] (1558?–86) was convicted of being a member of the Babington (Roman Catholic) conspiracy against Queen Elizabeth I. He wrote this poem in the Tower of London shortly before his execution:

Tichborne's Elegy

My prime of youth is but a frost of cares;
   My feast of joy is but a dish of pain;
My crop of corn is but a field of tares;
   And all my good is but vain hope of gain:
The day is past, and yet I saw no sun;
And now I live, and now my life is done.

My tale was heard, and yet it was not told;
   My fruit is fall'n, and yet my leaves are green;
My youth is spent, and yet I am not old;
   I saw the world, and yet I was not seen:
My thread is cut, and yet it is not spun;
And now I live, and now my life is done.

I sought my death, and found it in my womb;
   I looked for life, and saw it was a shade;
I trod the earth, and knew it was my tomb;
   And now I die, and now I was but made:
My glass is full, and now my glass is run;
And now I live, and now my life is done.

NOTE
1. An ancestor of Sir Roger Tichborne.

Poetic Justice / 1

The Convict's Song[1]

The Farewell
Farewell to old England the beautiful!
Farewell to my old pals as well!
Farewell to the famous Old Bailey,
Where I used for to cut sich a swell.

The Werdhick
These seving long years I've been serving,
And seving I've got for to stay,
All for bashing a bloke down our alley,
And' a' takin' his huxters[2] away!

The Complaint
There's the Captain wot is our Commanduer,
There's the Bosun and all the ship's crew,
There's the married as well as the single uns,
Knows wot we pore convicks go through.

The Suffering
It ain't 'cos they don't give us grub enough,
It ain't 'cos they don't give us clo'es:
It's a-cos all we light-fingered gentery
Goes about with a log on our toes.

The Prayer
Oh, had I the wings of a turtle dove,
Across the broad ocean I'd fly
Right into the arms of my Polly love
And on her soft bosum I'd lie!

Whitehall 5th February 1788

Sir,

His Majesty having been pleased
to give Directions that the Male Convicts
whose Names are in the Margin under
Sentence of Transportation in the Gaol at
Morpeth, should be removed from thence on
board the Dunkirk at Plymouth, and
committed to the Charge of Henry Bradley
Esqr. Overseer of the Convicts on board the
said Ship; I am commanded to signify to You
the King's Pleasure that You do cause the
said Convicts (if upon being examined by an
experienced Surgeon they shall be found free
from any putrid or infectious Distemper) to
be removed on board the said Ship, where they
are to remain until their Sentences can
be carried into Execution, or be otherwise
disposed of according to Law. I am
Sir, Your most obedient humble Servt.

Sydney

(margin names:)
William Stephenson.
Peter Gilles.
otherwise James
Daglish, otherwise
John Potts,
Ralph Stokoe.

Sheriff of Northumberland.

bloody

versicles

220

The Morrell

Now, all you young wi-counts and duchesses,
Take warning by wot I've to say,
And mind all your own wot you touches is,
Or you'll jine us in Botinny Bay![3]

NOTES

1. This song, with "Ri-chooral, ri-chooral, Oh!" embellishments, was featured in Dion Boucicault's *Janet Pride,* staged at the Adelphi Theatre, London, in 1855.

2. Huxters = money.

3. Transportation to the Australian convict settlements ended in 1868.

Prison Graffiti

One more month then out we go,
Then for feed of Hot Coco.
Fried Bread and Steak, Plenty of Beer,
Better tuck than we gets here.

☞

Cheer up, boys, down with sorrow:
Beef today, Soup tomorrow.

☞

Oh who can tell the panes I feel,
A poor and harmless sailor,
I miss my grog and every meal;
Here comes the blooming jailor.

☞

When I get out I do intend
My future life to try and mend,
For sneaking's a game that does not pay;
You are bound to get lagged, do what you may.
Written by one who knows it to his sorrow,
Who expects 12 months for only a borrow.

☞

For seven long years have I served them,
And seven long years I have to stay,
For meeting a bloke in our alley
And taking his ticker away.

Goodbye, Lucy dear,
I'm parted from you for seven long year.

ALF JONES

(Underneath the above:)

If Lucy dear is like most gals,
She'll give few sighs or moans,
But soon will find among your pals
Another Alfred Jones.

☛

Millbank for thick shins and graft at the pump,
Broadmoor for all laggs who go off their chump,
Brixton for good bread and cocoa with fat,
Dartmoor for bad grub, but plenty of chat;
Portsmouth a blooming bad place for hard work,
Chatham on Sunday gives four ounces of pork,
Portland is the worst place of the lot for to joke in,
For fetching a lagging there's no place like Woking.

NOTES

All of these verses were noted by the Reverend J. W. Horsley, last chaplain to Clerkenwell Prison, which opened in 1616, closed in 1877, and was demolished in 1890. Though not in verse, some one-prompting-another graffiti are worth noting, I think:

My mother made me a homosexual.

(Underneath the above:)

If I buy her the wool, will she make me one too?

A few years ago, while getting petrol at a filling station in Liverpool, I saw, scribbled on a wall of the forecourt, the demand:

FREE EAMON O'BLOGGS [or some such name].

(Underneath the above:)

—with every 2 liters of Shell Super Oil.

The Faking Boy

Air: The Minstrel Boy

The faking boy to the crap is gone,
At the nubbling chit you'll find him;
The hempen cord they have girded on,
And his elbows pinned behind him.
"Smash my glim!" cried the reg'lar card,
"Though the girl you love betrays you,
Don't split, but die both game and hard,
And grateful pals shall praise you!"

The bolt it fell—a jerk, a strain!
The sheriffs fled asunder;
The faking boy ne'er spoke again,
For they pulled his legs from under.
And there he dangles on the tree,
That soul of love and bravery!
Oh, that such men should victims be
Of law, and law's vile knavery!

JACK FIREBLOOD,
Flowers of Hemp, 1841

Crap = hanging; nubbling chit = gallows; glim = light (so "smash my glim" would seem to be a member of the family of expletives to which "blow me down" belongs).

Berry's Advice

After measuring and weighing a condemned man, James Berry, the nineteenth-century hangman,[1] used to hand him a piece of paper with these lines upon it:

My brother—sit and think,
While yet on earth some hours are left to thee;
Kneel to thy God, who does not from thee shrink,
And lay thy sins on Christ, who died for thee.

He rests His wounded hand
With loving kindness on thy sin-stained brow
And says, "Here at thy side I ready stand
To make thy scarlet sins as white as snow.

I did not shed My blood
For sinless angels good and pure and true;
For hopeless sinners flowed that crimson blood,
My heart's blood ran for you, My son, for you.

Though thou hast grieved Me sore,
My arms of mercy still are open wide,
I still hold open Heaven's shining door.
Come, then, take refuge in My wounded side.

Men shun thee—but not I.
Come close to me, I love My erring sheep.
My blood can cleanse thy sins of blackest dye.
I understand, if thou can'st only weep.

Words fail thee—never mind.
The Savior can read e'en a sigh, a tear;

I came, sin-stricken hearts to heal and bind,
And died to save thee; to My heart thou'rt dear.

Come now: the time is short.
Longing to pardon and to bless I wait.
Look up to Me, My sheep so dearly bought,
And say, 'Forgive me ere it is too late.' "

NOTE

1. Following the arrest, in 1902, of George Chapman (Severin Klosowski) for the murder of his three common-law wives, a copy of Berry's biography was found among his possessions. In the Introduction to *Trial of George Chapman* (Hodge, 1930), H. L. Adam writes: "A paragraph describing this particular find appeared in the newspapers, and was noticed by Berry, who . . . appealed to the police to keep all reference to his book out of the case, explaining that he wished to be entirely dissociated from it. He had, he said, destroyed all the copies remaining in his possession, and all others which he could find. Although he gave no reason for his eager desire for the total obliteration of his own creative work, it is possible that he may have sought to forget entirely his grim professional experiences. At any rate, he was not disturbed, for in the evidence the police made no reference to the book."

Adam writes of Chapman's second victim: "She was buried at Lynn, in Cheshire, five miles from her native village. On her grave there is a mourning card which reads: 'In loving memory of Bessie Chapman, wife of George Chapman, and the daughter of Thomas P. and Betsy Taylor, who died February 13, 1901, aged 36 years, and was interred at Lynn, February 15.' Then follows this verse, which savors very strongly of Chapman and may have been his own composition:

> Farewell, my friends, fond and dear,
> Weep not for me one single tear;
> For all that was and could be done,
> You plainly see my time was come."

In the "Hanging: From a Business Point of View" chapter of his book (*My Experiences as an Executioner,* reprinted by David & Charles in 1971, with an introduction, etc., by Jonathan Goodman, Berry wrote: "I am not ashamed of my calling, because I consider that if it is right for men to be executed (which I believe it is, in murder cases), it is right that the office of executioner should be held respectable. . . . When I first took up the work I was in the habit of applying to the Sheriff of the County whenever a murderer was condemned to death. I no longer consider it necessary to apply for work in England, because I am now well known, but I still send a simple address card, as below, when an execution in Ireland is announced."

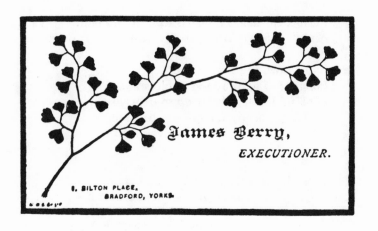

James Berry,

EXECUTIONER.

1, BILTON PLACE,
BRADFORD, YORKS.

The Ballad of Sam Hall

(Victorian popular song)

Oh, my name it is Sam Hall, Samuel Hall.
Oh, my name it is Sam Hall, Samuel Hall.
Oh, my name it is Sam Hall—and I hate you one and all;
You're a gang of muckers all—
>> Damn your eyes!

Oh, they say I killed a man, so they said.
Oh, they say I killed a man, so they said.
For I hit him on the 'ead with a bloody great lump
    of lead.
Oh, I left him there for dead,
>> Damn 'is eyes!

Oh, they put me into quod, into quod.
Oh, they put me into quod, into quod.
Oh, they put me into quod all for killing of that sod,
They did—so 'elp me God—
>> Damn their eyes!

Oh, the parson 'e did come, 'e did come.
Oh, the parson 'e did come, 'e did come.
Oh, the parson 'e did come and 'e looked so bloody glum
And he talked of Kingdom Come—
>> Damn 'is eyes!

So hup the steps I go, very slow.
So hup the steps I go, very slow.
So hup the steps I go and you muckers down below
Are standing in a row,
>> Damn your eyes!

I sees Molly in the crowd, in the crowd.
I sees Molly in the crowd, in the crowd.
I sees Molly in the crowd, so I holler out aloud,
"Now ain't you bleedin' proud,
                    Damn your eyes!"

And now I 'ears the bell, 'ears the bell.
And now I 'ears the bell, 'ears the bell.
And it is my funeral knell, and I'll meet you all in Hell,
And I 'opes you frizzle well.
                    Damn your eyes!

Song of the Scaffold

In *The Newgate Garland*, published by Desmond Harmsworth
in 1932, W. L. Hanchant stated that "only a few months since,
outside a public-house near the 'Factory' [Pentonville Prison],"
he had heard a busker singing this song:

> Hark to the clinking of hammers,
> Hark to the driving of nails,
> The men are erecting a gallows
> In one of her Majesty's gaols.
> A life, human life's to be taken,
> Which the crowd and the hangman hail,
> For the men are erecting a scaffold
> In one of her Majesty's gaols.
>
> 'Tis midnight—without is dead silence—
> The doomed wretch in agony moans,
> But the clattering din of the hammers
> Is drowning the poor wretch's groans.
> The chaplain now earnestly prayeth
> To the God of all mercy for him,
> But his mind on his misery strayeth,
> For his cup is full up to the brim.
>
> "O pray while you may to your Maker,
> His mercy, not justice, implore,"
> Said the priest while hot tears filled his eyelids,
> And his choked voice could utter no more.
> "You ask me to pray," said the felon,
> "But no one e'er showed me the way;
> 'Tis too late, 'tis too late now to teach me,
> I can't understand what you say."

Hark! hark! the death bell is tolling,
The gallows at last is in view,
The prisoner, pale, ghastly, sinking,
To the chaplain has waved an adieu.
His strong frame in agony quivers,
His breast—see how wildly it heaves,
His arms, oh how closely they're pinioned,
The hangman himself almost grieves.

Hush! hark! the death bell is tolling,
Dragoons with drawn swords are below,
The prisoner seems to be praying,
'Tis a scene of heart-anguish and woe;
There are crowds in the streets, men and women,
The war steeds are prancing about,
The windows are thronged with spectators,
Hark! a buzz and a wave and a shout.

The rope round his neck is adjusted
(Man's vengeance, how fearful thou art!).
His head now is covered, and horror
Strikes every man to the heart.
The dead bolt is drawn! he is plunging
In air, what a terrible tale!
His soul has been borne to its maker,
His corpse taken back to the gaol.

Poetic Justice / 2

The Culprit[1]

The night my father got me
  His mind was not on me;
He did not plague his fancy
  To muse if I should be
  The son you see.

The day my mother bore me
  She was a fool and glad,
For all the pain I cost her,
  That she had borne the lad
  That borne she had.

My mother and my father
  Out of the light they lie;
The warrant would not find them,
  And here 'tis only I
  Shall hang so high.

Oh let not man remember
  The soul that God forgot,
But fetch the county kerchief
  And noose me in the knot,
  And I will rot.

For so the game is ended
  That should not have begun;
My father and my mother
  They had a likely son;
  And I have none.

        A. E. HOUSMAN

NOTE

1. This poem was quoted by Clarence Darrow during his closing speech for the defense at the trial of Nathan Leopold and Richard Loeb for the kidnapping and murder of fourteen-year-old Robert Franks (Chicago, 1924).

Abolitionist View

Hang Down Your Head and Die, devised by David Wright, was first produced at the Oxford Playhouse on 11 February 1964. The show was conceived and executed in a circus framework, within which the condemned man was represented by a white-faced clown, the hangman by the strong man, and authority in general by two ringmasters. At the beginning of the show, backed by a projection of the caption "Royal Commission on Capital Punishment 1948–53," the whole company entered for a "typical, breezy musical opener":

There's Gonna be a Commission

Capital punishment is not the same
Since it has ceased as a public game.
Now what they want is peace and quiet—
No traditional crowds, no traditional riots.

Chorus:
There's gonna be a Commission;
King George has given permission
To find the way to punish today
In best British tradition.

In 1930 the last Commission said,
The death penalty itself should be dead;
But we know what a commission decide
The British Government like to over-ride.

(Chorus repeat)

Now once again there is hope,
Guilty men will escape guilty rope,

For in mercy and justice one sees no point
When one has one's neck out of joint.

(Chorus repeat)

When the Commission finishes you will see
Eleven members get the O.B.E.
Will this be the last, or will it be the same?—
Yet another British party game.

ROBERT HEWISON and VASHTI BUNYAN

Later on in the first part of the show, the white-faced clown sang a song by David Wood about the advantages of gas, which ended:

On dilute sulphuric acid falls
Solid cyanide in cute little balls.
I want gas zzz zzzz. . . .
I want gas zzz zzzz.
I want something that killed the Jews en masse:
I want gas. . . . I want gas.
What a gas!

The stage directions for "An Innocent Man is Never Hanged" read:

The song is sung by a clown and the two ringmasters in the music-hall style. As the singers exit, the girls appear on the opposite side of the stage picked out by a follow-spot. The girls' speeches should be coyly spoken with big, bright smiles.

CLOWN: I have often heard it said
            By the wealthy and well-bred
            That the scales of British justice are fairly bal-
               anced.
            Now this may not be new,
            But I believe it to be true,
            And mistakes can never happen—to me or even
               you.

CHORUS: An innocent man is never hanged,
            Mistakes are never made;

So if you didn't commit the crime,
You needn't be afraid.

GIRL 1: In 1953 Derek Bentley was hanged at Wandsworth Jail for the murder of a police officer. Curiously, this police officer was actually shot by Bentley's accomplice, Christopher Craig. Bentley was in fact under arrest at the time the fatal shot was fired.

ACTUALITY: *(indicates the edited, recorded opinions of the general public)* He pleaded to the last moment that he wasn't guilty. He said he didn't know that the other person had a gun. And even in the last two hours before he went on the scaffold, he still said he didn't have a gun. He didn't know—but I suppose that doesn't make any difference to the law, does it?

GIRL 1: But English law regards the accomplice in crime as a principal, so both Bentley and Craig were found guilty of the murder of the police officer. Craig, being under eighteen years of age, was sentenced to be detained during Her Majesty's pleasure. Derek Bentley was hanged by the neck until dead.

CHORUS: An innocent man is never hanged,
Mistakes are never made;
So if you didn't commit the crime,
You needn't be afraid.

GIRL 2: On the 15th March 1957 Burton Abbot was condemned to death for the murder of a fourteen-year-old girl. He was placed in the lethal gas chamber of California State Prison. The time was 11:15. At 11:18 he breathed the first whiffs of gas. At 11:20 the Secretary for the Committee of Reprieves 'phoned the prison with a stay of execution. The call was a little late as the secretary had tried to 'phone the governor direct, but as at the time he was out sailing, there was a delay before he contacted the prison direct. Abbot was hastily removed from the lethal gas chamber, but unfortunately he was already dead.

CHORUS: An innocent man is never hanged,
Mistakes are never made;
So if you didn't commit the crime,
You needn't be afraid.

GIRL 3: In 1936 Mrs. Bryant was hanged for the murder of her husband by arsenic poisoning. Evidence was submitted to show that a tin said to have contained arsenic has been burned by her in a copper fire. The ashes were analyzed and were found to contain 149.6 parts of arsenic in a million, which the expert said proved that arsenic had been put on the fire. But another learned man, a professor at the Imperial College of Science and Technology, and one of the greatest of our authorities on fuels and their residues, said that *all* coal ash contains arsenic. The court of appeal refused to hear his evidence, and Mrs. Bryant was hanged by the neck until dead.

CHORUS: An innocent man is never hanged,
Mistakes are never made;
So if you didn't commit the crime,
You needn't be afraid.

GIRL 4: Timothy Evans of 10 Rillington Place, a mentally retarded van-driver, was charged in October 1949 with murdering his wife and child and executed on November 8th in the same year. On the 15th of July, 1953, John Christie, also of 10 Rillington Place, was executed for the murder of six women, one of whom was Mrs. Evans.[1]

CHORUS: An innocent man is never hanged,
Mistakes are never made;
So if you didn't commit the crime,
You needn't be afraid.
If there's anyone in doubt, I say, "Wake up, you fool,

TEACHER: Today Ruth Ellis was hanged. Not only myself but many of my colleagues were faced with the effect of this upon the boys and girls that we teach. The school was in a ferment. There were some children who had waited outside the prison gates: some claimed to have seen the execution from their windows: others spoke with fascinated horror about the technique of hanging a female.

SLIDE: Hanratty is hanged, April 1962 (*Projected during actuality only*).

ACTUALITY: They made models of him or graves and they had a countdown to the point when he died. And at the time when he died they destroyed the models or burnt the graves or destroyed them in some way. And before he died—about five minutes before he died—they'd draw pictures of the gallows, and as each minute went by they added a bit more to it until after the five minutes were up they'd drawn a gallows with a model hanging from it.

TEACHER: My colleagues and I agree that if there is one argument which weighs above all others, then it is the dreadful influence it has. For not only was Ruth Ellis hanged today, but hundreds of children were a little corrupted.

SINGER: In Jerusalem each day in the temple of Jehovah,
The Jews would go a pigeon for to kill;
Jesus Christ one day this practice tried to stop,
But in England we carry on still.
For a week before the day that we celebrate his birth,
Two murderers died hanging from a tree;
It was men who died that day, not pigeons bought for gold,
Killed in the name of you and me.

2 SINGERS: At eight o'clock one morning in December '63,
            The prison bells told their weary tale,
            And Russell Pascoe died that day in Horfield
                town
            And Whitty in Winchester Jail.

            They killed a lonely farmer and no mercy did
                they show
            When they battered in his head and let him lie,
            But an eye for an eye and a tooth for a tooth,
            So the law said that both of them should die.

            Well, we've had our eye and we've had our tooth,
            And their lodging is now the cold ground,
            With no headstones to crown their bones
            To show where we laid them both down.

            Where we had one corpse we now have three,
            And over each the graveyard thistle waves,
            And many gone before and others to be born
            Will end their lives to fill dishonored graves.

            Black is the color and silence is the sound
            And nothing is the number when you die,
            And the mountains are sand and the seas are all
                dry
            When the light has gone down from the sky.

                                              DAVID WOOD

Another song by David Wood, "The English Way to Die,"
was sung in the style of Noel Coward. The following are
extracts:

            As we walk towards the gallows
            To escape we do not try;
            With a smile upon our faces,
            We hold our heads up high.
            Our upper lip is stiff as we say our last goodbye:
            It's the English way to die.

We await our final moment
As we look towards the sky,
And ne'er a tear or trickle
Falls from our unflinching eye.
To go in true blue fashion we must keep our kerchiefs dry:
It's the English way to die.

Our necks in the noose now
The appointed time draws near.
There's just one thing that we're thinking:
Don't forsake the old school tie.
A man's about to kill us; we ask no reason why:
It's the English way to die.

NOTE

1. A mistake; see page 115.

A Medico-Legal Expert

Scotland has produced more than its fair share of forensic scientists. One of the best known was John Glaister (1856–1932)[1], who figured in many sensational Scottish criminal trials of the early years of this century. He was professor of Forensic Medicine at Glasgow University, 1898–1931.

I am indebted to my friend, the late Professor J. Henry Dible,[2] for recalling "The Ballad of John Glaister," which was current circa 1908 when he was a student of Glaister's. Many contributed to it, including O. H. Mavor ("James Bridie," the playwright).

Oh, I am the marvel of Medical Ju.,
A fact which I hope to impress upon you,
And I never get flurried whatever I do,
For I'm the great Professor John Glaister—
Just bear that in mind and you're sure to get through.

If a stair-head encounter be raging apace,
If your mother-in-law bite a chunk off your face,
I can tell from the notes that I take on the case,
I can tell from the lesions I find on the body
The time and the tool and the manner and place.

If a mummified foetus be found up your lum,
If your wife stick a poker red-hot up your bum,
If you playfully oscar an affable chum,
Mr. Justice Hawkins and me, we agree,
That into our hands you will certainly come.

If you fall by mischance down the w.c.,
If your penis and scrotum you thread through a key,
You'd better bring round all your troubles to me

And I'll set them right, and besides I am bound
By professional vows to the strictest q.t.

If your wife takes a pill with intent to abort,
It's cases like this which I hold as my forte,
And I furnish a medico-legal report
In terms of Vict. 2 cap. 1 section 60,
With details that necessitate clearing the court.

I examine for Crown in all cases of rape,
I measure the parts with a forty-foot tape;
The garments for seminal stains I scrape,
And I catch each giddy wee spermatozoa
And never let one little bugger escape.

Unhappy cryptorchids all flock to my door,
And hubbies who fancy they've married a whore;
Of imperforate hymens I widen the bore
And anesthetize hyper-aesthetic vaginas
"In ways I have previously detailed before."

Mid high exhumations I sniff for a clue,
In columns of water I hunt for them too,
For everything fishy and foetid and blue
Is all in the line of Professor John Glaister—
"And remember, the converse is equally true."

If you happen to die in a manner that's queer,
If you're struck down by lightning or poisoned by beer,
With the fiscal's permission I probe and I peer
Into "all the organs of all the cavities,"
Reserving a portion for adipocere.

If your son aged eleven has large, hairy balls,
And fornicates freely with imbecile molls,
For my medico-legal attention he calls,
And I publish his quite preternatural penis
In picturesque pose on my lecture-room walls.

The P.M.'s the place where I show forth my art
As I carefully carve each particular part,

And the copious notes which I take from the start
Can only be used to "refresh my memory,"
And in manner and style they're especially smart.

When the High Court comes round, I am cock of the walk,
'Neath examining counsel I'm firm as a rock,
For I state my case without hurry or flurry,
And I hold with the Judge in untechnical talk,
As I always refer to the penis as cock.

So bring out your swipes of frankincense and myrrh,
Bring Indian coral and Eskimo fur,
Bring harlots, bring whiskies, and kick up a stir,
For I am a special old pal of Jehovah's,
And angels and cherubims all call me "Sir."

Now please keep in mind I'm a self-made M.D.,
A D.P.H. Cambridge and F.R.S.E.,
And if I should live to the next century,
The King will create me the first Baron Glaister,
A thing which is fitting, I'm sure you'll agree.

NOTES

1. Not to be confused with his son (see footnote, page 113), who was Emeritus Professor of Forensic Medicine at Glasgow University, 1931–62.

2. He was one of the expert medical witnesses for the defense at the trial of William Herbert Wallace.

Acknowledgments

Many people have helped me by supplying examples of chrymes and information about cases, and I am particularly grateful to the following:

George Burnett.

Richard Whittington-Egan.

J. Allison; Rev. Claude A. Bartle; Albert Borowitz; Richard Boyd-Carpenter; Ivan Butler; Peter Cotes; R. M. H. Cree; Professor J. Henry Dible; Basil Donne-Smith; Harold Ford; A. Frowd-Jones, editor of the *Bournemouth Times;* Joe Gaute; Mrs. Bessie Hale; Archie Harradine of the Players' Theatre; Walter Henderson; Robert F. Hussey (USA); Ludovic Kennedy; Roger Lovell; Thomas M. McDade (USA); Hector Munro; Monty Norman; Miss Olive Peden; Christopher Pulling; L. N. Radcliffe, editor-in-chief of the Whitethorn Press Ltd.; Sidney Smith; Miss Joan Sterndale Bennett of the Players' Theatre; Julian Symons; Miss Molly Tibbs; Miss E. Waugh; John M. Williamson; Mrs. Ann Winning; David Wood; David Wright.

Miss Muriel H. Simpson, librarian and curator, Berwick-upon-Tweed; K. F. Stanesby, borough librarian and keeper, Burton-upon-Trent; E. R. C. Lintott, library manager of the *Daily Mirror;* A. E. Brown, director of libraries, Enfield; Mrs. Ruth Noyes, librarian of the English Folk Dance and Song Society; Mme. C. Launois, librarian of the Institut Français du Royaume-Uni; P. Henchy, director of the National Library of Ireland; Miss Bridget Yates, assistant curator of the London Museum; John P. Baker, executive assistant at the New York Public Library; Miss Marie C. Jordan, librarian of George Outram & Co. Ltd.; G. E. Thornber, director, Rochdale Public Libraries and Arts Services; Miss Jessie Dobson, recorder of the Museum of the Royal College of Surgeons of England; the staff of the reference department of *The Stage;* William J. Skillern, head of Reference Services, Stockport; T. Berentemfel, librarian of *The Sun.*

My thanks are due to the following for permission to reproduce copyright material:

Michael Brown—for "You Can't Chop your Poppa Up in Massachusetts"; K. F. Dallas Ltd.—for "Derek Bentley," © 1953 by Karl Dallas; Monty Norman—for "The Ballad of Doctor Crippen"; Ewan MacColl—for "Go Down, You Murderers"; Planetary-Nom (London) Ltd.—for "Strange Fruit" by Lewis Allen, © 1959 by E. B. Marks Music Corporation; Essex Music Ltd.—for "The Lament of Inglebert Ralph Thole," "The Prostitutes' Padre," "The Fight Goes On," "All That Gas," "An Innocent Man is Never Hanged," "The English Way to Die" by David Wood, and for "There's Gonna be a Commission" by Robert Hewison and Vashti Bunyan.

Finally, thanks to the Borowitz True Crime Collection, Department of Special Collections and Archives, Kent State University Libraries, for supplying the additional artwork.

Index

Authors quoted or referred to in the text are either protagonists or observers; the names of the latter are printed in *italics* in this index.

Bloody Versicles
was composed in 10/13 ITC New Baskerville
on a Xyvision system with Linotronic output
by BookMasters, Inc.;
printed by sheet-fed offset
on 60-pound Glatfelter Natural acid-free stock,
and notch bound in signatures
with paper covers printed in two colors on 12-point
coated-one-side stock with film lamination
by Thomson-Shore, Inc.;
designed by Will Underwood;
and published by
The Kent State University Press
KENT, OHIO 44242